If you've never been asked why the Bible ... you've never asked that question yourself, you should. And this brief, non-technical volume will be of great help in beginning to formulate an answer. With both humor and humility, Trevor Sutton guides readers through some of the most common objections to Scripture's trustworthiness, answering each winsomely and wittily—and pastorally. Highly recommended for youth and adult Bible studies and for all parish libraries.

—*Rev. Dr. Korey Maas, assistant professor of history,*
Hillsdale College, Michigan

Trevor Sutton has provided a wealth of information and explanation that is a needed antidote for our time. *Why Should I Trust the Bible?* identifies and responds to the many baseless but constant arguments against the authority of the Bible. Rev. Sutton's work is easy to read and well-argued yet brief and to the point. The excursus after each chapter offers enlightening and powerful comparisons between the Bible and other texts. The question-and-answer section for each chapter is also a very helpful resource for both readers and teachers. I anticipate referencing this work often in the courses I teach and would suggest it as required reading for Lutheran high schools and universities.

—*Rev. Dr. Michael Eschelbach, professor of New Testament,*
Concordia University, Irvine

Why Should I Trust the Bible? demonstrates a style of writing our churches need. Trevor Sutton removes the jargon from theology so that all the members of Christ's Church, lay and clergy, can learn more about the truth of God's Word in a way we can easily understand and put to use in our daily life and witness. The title poses a question, Why should I trust the Bible?, and Pastor Sutton's answers will bless individual reading, study groups, and sermons.

—*Rev. Dr. Dale A. Meyer, president,*
Concordia Seminary, St. Louis, Missouri

Many have been troubled by the glib, shallow, and often ill-informed challenges to the Christian faith that permeate our society, even in its most well-respected secular news and information media. This is a book for any layperson who has been bothered by the sincere—and, at times, cynical—

but misleading repetition of these challenges. Rev. Sutton explains the basic issues in straightforward, understandable language without getting bogged down in technicalities, which can be left to later exploration of particular issues. This book is the entry point for anyone who wishes to fortify their defense of the Christian faith with knowledge of the facts. Its inclusion of discussion items for each chapter makes it a convenient way to probe the issues with others who are also seeking to grow in their knowledge, or they can be used simply for one's own review and as a spur for further study.

—*Rev. Dr. Andrew Steinmann, distinguished professor of theology and Hebrew, Concordia University Chicago*

In a time in the world when there are so many more questions than answers, this book speaks with great clarity and great precision about the reliability of the Holy Scriptures. While the thinking is deep and detailed, the writing is warm and pastoral. The author has a simple formula that leads the reader to understanding God's plan of salvation: Grace + Faith = Salvation. Simple is good! Thank you, Pastor Sutton, for this fine work.

—*Rev. Timothy M. Klinkenberg, senior pastor, St. John's Lutheran Church, Orange, California*

Where can we put our trust in today's "headline equals truth," fast-paced, quick-scrolling culture? Having spent my career engaging in the digital space, I see how the onslaught of secular humanism relentlessly berates the Christian worldview. As the attacks reign down upon us, it's only natural for Bible-believing Christians to have moments where we pause and ask: Is this all true? Can the Bible that proclaims our Savior be trusted? In *Why I Should Trust the Bible?*, Rev. Sutton takes a number of myths that seek to discredit the Bible and places them on the table for discussion. Chapter by chapter, he carefully dissects each claim in detail and counters them with solid biblical truth. By taking the time to examine each claim, Sutton strengthens our confidence in the Bible and equips us to more thoughtfully share the truth with our family, friends, and neighbors in truth and love whether online or offline. I pray that this is the first in a series of apologetic books.

—*Seth R. Hinz, assistant to the president—web and media director, LCMS Michigan District*

WHY SHOULD I TRUST THE BIBLE?

A. TREVOR SUTTON

CONCORDIA PUBLISHING HOUSE · SAINT LOUIS

Published by Concordia Publishing House
3558 S. Jefferson Ave., St. Louis, MO 63118-3968
1-800-325-3040 • www.cph.org

Manufactured in the United States of America

Library of Congress Cataloging-in-Publication Data
Names: Sutton, A. Trevor, author.
Title: Why should I trust the Bible? / A. Trevor Sutton.
Description: St. Louis, MO : Concordia Publishing House, 2016.

Identifiers: LCCN 2016024327 (print) | LCCN 2016024428 (ebook) | ISBN
      9780758651846 | ISBN 9780758651853 ()

Subjects: LCSH: Bible--Inspiration. | Bible--Evidences, authority, etc.
Classification: LCC BS480 .S79 2016 (print) | LCC BS480 (ebook) | DDC
      220.1--dc23
LC record available at https://lccn.loc.gov/2016024327

1 2 3 4 5 6 7 8 9 10   25 24 23 22 21 20 19 18 17 16

CONTENTS

FOREWORD

By Rev. Dr. Patrick T. Ferry
President of Concordia University
Ann Arbor and Wisconsin

The Bible is utterly reliable, and the truth that Holy Scripture teaches can and should be embraced with complete confidence. Of course, many—perhaps most—in our day and age would regard such an attitude about the Bible as risible and even ridiculous. For Christians, particularly young followers of Christ, the challenges of living in what some call the "post-Church" era are intensifying. While following faithfully as a disciple of Jesus has never been an easy trek, nor should we expect it to be, the path is becoming more treacherous at every turn. Efforts to marginalize or even jettison Christian influence in our society are gaining startling momentum. In ways both subtle and overt, opponents have sought to compromise Christianity's teaching and eliminate its impact by doing damage to the foundation of the faith. If the source is cut off, the flow is halted. Not surprisingly, therefore, the Bible—the foundation of our faith and the source of all that we believe, teach, and confess—is a main target for those who would discredit Christianity.

"The Bible cannot be trusted" is the mantra of deniers and detractors who seek to undermine the Church's teaching. Critiques and complaints come from all quarters, leaving those who espouse traditional Christian viewpoints encircled by opposition. The pivot on which that opposition turns, however, is the exact point on which the Church either stands or falls. Can the Bible be trusted? Those who insist that it cannot mount a pile of arguments designed to cause the faithful to lose their footing. After all, if the Bible cannot be relied on as a firm foundation and solid source, then all of Christianity's claims about truth become slippery and slide away. Absolute truth is a concept inherent to Christian faith but not much in step with the relativist worldview that is so much in vogue. Truth assertions of the Bible seem groundless in a relativistic culture.

It is naïve merely to reassure ourselves that this opposition will do the Church and followers of Christ no real harm. Regrettably, Christians of all ages, but especially our youth, often are left wondering what to believe about the Bible. Worse, certainly, is the unfortunate reality that wondering about the Bible's credibility has led so many to wander from the truth. Young people leave the Church and repudiate the Bible and its teaching in alarming numbers. The tough issues outsiders raise are sometimes puzzling. Our own honest attempts to grapple with uncertainties can be perplexing. Amid the many voices that would say otherwise, God's people need to hear clear and convincing arguments that show that the Bible can be trusted and that the truth the Bible teaches ought to be trusted absolutely.

In *Why Should I Trust the Bible?*, Trevor Sutton provides a thoughtful and cogent response to the questions about Holy Scripture that opponents raise. Pastorally and persuasively, he also treats the troubling concerns about God's Word that we who are believers may struggle with ourselves. A defense without being defensive, Pastor Sutton's winsome witness to the complete reliability of the Bible as the very Word of God will engage readers on every page, equipping followers of Christ with keen and credible insights.

Because skeptics and scoffers raise doubts from every imaginable direction, Pastor Sutton anticipates and addresses all sorts of misgivings without shying away. Setting up "straw man" arguments only to knock them down would offer little enduring benefit to a young person grappling with hard questions about what to believe and whether the Bible is believable. Therefore, Pastor Sutton does not omit criticisms or critics' best attempts to debunk the veracity of the Bible. Instead, he allows each chapter to represent various aspects of the range of opposition. Is the Bible merely mythological? Is Scripture fraught with errors and discrepancies? How does the biblical account square with history? What makes the books of the Bible any more reliable than other texts from the same period that were called "Gospels" or were supposedly attributed to the apostles? Is the Bible even relevant to our time and place? Given differences in translations and interpretations, how can we be sure about what we read? Doesn't the Bible advocate socially unacceptable and even reprehensible points of view? Are not many of the claims of Scripture simply beyond belief? Neither these nor the many other questions that are considered in the text and included in the study questions at the end of each chapter are exhaustive. Those who reject the reliability of the Bible and deny the trustworthiness of the truth may not be convinced, and their questions will not cease. But, questions never really derail the truth. Questions present an opportunity to explain the truth and to do so in confidence that our foundation is sure and our source is pure. The Bible is reliable, not because Pastor Sutton or anyone else says so, but because it is God's Word. The answers we find in the Word to even the most challenging questions are not only plausible, but also completely convincing.

Central to the book's thesis, and central to the truth that the Bible asserts, is the truth about Jesus Christ—"the way, and the truth, and the life" (John 14:6). What John writes toward the end of His Gospel is applicable to the entirety of the Bible: "These are written so that you may believe that Jesus is the Christ, the Son of God, and that by believing you may have life in His name" (20:31). Other allegations that supposedly negate the Bible's trustworthiness also receive Pastor Sutton's dutiful and careful attention. His response draws not only on the Scriptures themselves, but also on illuminating examples and thought-provoking comparisons from history and literature. Who would ever have imagined that the Gettysburg Address or the writings of William Faulkner might reinforce the trustworthiness of the Bible? Pastor Sutton's resourceful methodology aims not to entertain but to engage us in fresh ways. However, if we can't trust what the Bible teaches regarding Jesus Christ, then none of the other questions people pose matter much at all. By contrast, if the Bible provides a truthful witness about the person and work of Jesus Christ, much of the rest begins to fall into place. Since the Bible was "written so that [we] may believe that Jesus is the Christ, the Son of God, and that believing [we] may have life in His name" (John 20:31), there is much at stake in answering the question "Can I trust the Bible?"

Pastor Sutton understands what is at stake. He is a loving *Seelsorger*, a faithful shepherd who cares for the souls of people. Confusion and uncertainty are not good for our souls. A world without truth, and a life without Christ—who is Himself the Truth—is a world and life bereft of hope. Many lost souls amble hopelessly about in this broken world. Sutton's book may not satisfy the severest critic, but this shepherd reaches out to a different audience—God's people whose hope is built on Jesus Christ who loves us. This we know, for the Bible tells us so. A hymnwriter makes the same point this way: "How firm a foundation, O saints of the Lord, Is laid for your faith in His excellent Word" (*Lutheran Service Book* 728:1). Should you trust the Bible? Absolutely, and here is why. . . .

ACKNOWLEDGMENTS

Iron sharpens iron, and one man sharpens another.
(Proverbs 27:17)

God has used many people to sharpen my knowledge of Scripture. This book would not have been written without these individuals in my life. I praise God for their diligent and faithful sharpening of me.

My family has been a steadfast encouragement and support to me. God has used them to inscribe truth on my heart and mind. They keep me sharp and embolden me to press on in the Lord. My wife, Elizabeth, is my endlessly patient and supportive bride. My daughters, Grace and Hannah, are truly gifts from God. Their love and prayers keep me going.

My teachers have worked tirelessly to sharpen this otherwise dull instrument. I am indebted to the faculty of Concordia University, Ann Arbor, and especially the theology department. I would particularly like to thank Charles Schulz and Philip Penhallegon for dutifully teaching me biblical languages. I am also thankful for the exegetical faculty at Concordia Seminary in St. Louis. I would particularly like to thank James Voelz and Jeff Kloha for their influence on my understanding of hermeneutics.

My partners in ministry continue to keep me sharp in my reading of Scripture. I am blessed by brother pastors—Dave Davis, Zerit

Yohannes, David Maier, Mark Bushuiakovish, John Hile, Ben Vogel, Eric Ekong, Ryan Peterson, Ryan Winningham, Steve Newberg, Bill Wangelin—who keep me accountable in proclaiming the Gospel. My congregation, St. Luke Lutheran Church (Haslett, Michigan), encourages me daily by their love of God's Word and diligent study of Scripture.

Finally, I would like to thank everyone who helped in the editing of this book. Matthew Sauer provided a careful review of the manuscript. His brilliance and attention to detail greatly contributed to this project. Laura Lane at Concordia Publishing House is a truly wonderful editor and encouragement to me.

God has used many others not listed here. I am grateful for everyone whom the Lord uses to keep me sharp in my service to Him.

INTRODUCTION

Trust. It is not sold in stores. It is not a genetic trait bestowed on someone by previous generations. There is no life hack for instant trust. There is no app to download terabytes of trust in a few seconds. There is no way around it: trust is built. It rises from a foundation of truth. It grows slowly and painstakingly over years of steadfast honesty, reliability, and dependability. It holds together with the mortar of integrity. Trust is formed not all at once but over the course of many small interactions.

People work hard to build trust. Husbands and wives build trust by honoring the vows made to each other on their wedding day. Mothers and fathers build trust by keeping their children safe and properly fed. Christians build the trust of others by living a life fully aligned with their beliefs. Judges build trust by administering their office with integrity and upholding the law. Pastors build trust by practicing what they preach and living above reproach. Elected officials build trust by keeping campaign promises and faithfully serving constituents.

Just like individuals, organizations must also work hard to build trust. Companies build trust by consistently offering quality products and truthful advertising. Churches build trust by espousing truth and caring for the community. Schools build trust by offering a stellar education and graduating competent students. Governments build trust through fiscal responsibility and maintaining a safe community.

Trust is built. And trust is also broken. Although trust is built slowly, it is destroyed instantly. Lies, deceit, and exploitation disintegrate

Although trust is built slowly, it is destroyed instantly. trust in a moment. Misinformation, falsehood, and deception topple trust immediately. Husbands and wives break trust with a moment of infidelity and secrecy. Mothers and fathers break trust with only one careless decision. Christians break the trust of others with just one action contrary to their beliefs. Public figures break trust by a single abuse of power. Pastors break trust by pocketing church money and neglecting ministry responsibilities. Politicians break trust by taking bribes, promoting cronies, and misappropriating funds. Organizations break trust through negligence and falsehood. Churches and schools break trust by ignoring child abuse allegations. Trust is slowly built yet swiftly broken.

TRUSTING THE BIBLE

People trust in public figures and institutions. And people trust in the Bible. Not just a few people. Not just old people. Many people place their undivided trust in the Bible. Countless Christians lean on the Bible, trusting the words of God entirely.

Many other people have done exactly the opposite. Countless cynics have sought to break trust in the Bible. It has been barraged, besieged, and bombarded from every side. The ancient world saw myriad attacks on the Bible. Marcion of Sinope (AD 85–160) tried to reject the Old Testament by claiming it was incompatible with the New Testament. Gnostic communities claimed to have secret knowledge that had been excluded from the Bible. The Talmud, an ancient Jewish commentary, offered conflicting claims about the life of Jesus. In more recent history, the Age of Enlightenment tried to dismantle the authority of the Bible. Thomas Jefferson

(1743–1826) cut out every miracle that Jesus performed in order to create his Jefferson Bible. Every generation of believers has endured an attempt at breaking trust in the Bible.

Today is no different. People are still trying to break trust in the Bible. Modern scholars attempt to dismantle Scripture in any way possible: Historians claim that it is nothing more than a human text with a deeply political motive. Anthropologists argue that it is merely a record of rituals performed by an ancient people. Archaeologists assume that the historical claims of the Bible are in error. Sociologists assert that it is a religious text on the same plane as every other religious text. Today—as in every previous generation—people try to break trust in the Bible by questioning everything from the physical manuscripts and text to the formation of the biblical canon and how it is interpreted. The effort to deconstruct trust in the Bible is going on right now as you read this sentence.

Yet it is still standing.

Nothing has been able to break trust in the Bible. Every attempt has failed. Every effort to expose the Bible as fraudulent has ended in disappointment. Even the most brilliant scholars have been unsuccessful in dismantling trust in the Bible. It remains trustworthy after generations of attack. It is still historically accurate, textually reliable, and culturally relevant. It persists as the only viable source for Christian beliefs. It is as true for people living today as it was for previous generations. And it is still God's Word for all eternity.

The incessant effort to break trust in the Bible has had an unexpected result: every new analysis of Scripture further reveals its legitimacy. Each new discovery adds more to the already staggering evidence that the Bible is trustworthy. The unending attempts to *break* trust in the Bible have ironically worked to *build* trust in the Bible. Efforts to deconstruct Scripture have contributed only to its enduring power. Every generation has come to the same conclusion: you can still trust the Bible.

OVERVIEW

This book will build your trust in the Bible. And it will break your trust in other texts. You will find that the Bible is more credible than you had ever imagined. And you will find that other texts are far more questionable than you had ever imagined.

The first chapter anchors our trust in the Bible in Jesus Christ. His life, death, and resurrection provide the trustworthy foundation for every page in the Bible. The Bible would be simply a book like every other book in human history if it were not for Jesus. He is the foundation for our trust in the Bible.

The first chapter establishes Jesus as the foundation for our trust in the Bible; the subsequent chapters address numerous claims leveled against the Bible. These are common claims that individuals make for not trusting Scripture, and they range from arguing that there are errors in the text to calling it religious propaganda and downright racist:

- The Bible is merely a mythological story similar to Homer's *Odyssey*.

- Numerous flood stories exist from antiquity. The biblical story of Noah and the ark is a mixture of flood stories from other cultures.

- The Bible has so many errors and edits that it simply cannot be trusted.

- The Gospels disagree on even the most basic events in the life of Jesus.

- The Bible is clearly biased toward men. It was written by men and primarily for men.

- The Bible is racist and promotes slavery.

These claims, and many others, are addressed in the pages that follow. These are claims that you have heard from pessimistic professors, suspicious scholars, and antagonistic atheists. These claims have been made in popular television shows, academic debates, and other books. And some of these may be claims that you have personally brought against the Bible. These are questions and quandaries that anyone may have as they engage Scripture.

After the first chapter, every remaining chapter ends with a discussion on a nonbiblical text. These texts range from ancient to modern, secular to religious. The texts come from many different places, were penned by many different people, and were written for many different reasons. The texts discussed at the end of each chapter include the following:

- The *Epic of Gilgamesh*
- The Gettysburg Address
- The dramas of William Shakespeare
- The Gnostic Gospels
- Cautionary Children's Tales
- The writings of William Faulkner
- Encyclopedias
- The Book of Mormon

Despite the vast differences in these texts, they all have something in common: they come up lacking when compared to the Bible. This book will take the same rigorous methods used to critique the Bible and critique other well-respected texts. By doing so, it will show you how the Bible elicits an exceptional amount of trust. Other trusted texts fall apart when they are examined with the same level of scrutiny as Scripture. Every. Single. Time.

The manuscript evidence available for these texts is far smaller than the biblical manuscript evidence. The textual variants in these texts are far greater than the biblical textual variants. The historical discrepancies, unanswered questions, and insurmountable problems in these texts swell to a level that is far greater than any claims leveled against the Bible. These texts will provide a direct comparison with Scripture and show that it is trustworthy.

This book is a basic introduction to many different issues surrounding the Bible. The topics addressed in the pages that follow are not completely exhausted nor are they explored in extensive detail; biblical scholars have written thousands of texts on every individual claim discussed in this book. This is not the final word on any of these topics. Rather, this book provides a broad overview of the many claims made against the Bible. Since this book is not intended for biblical scholars, footnotes have been kept to a minimum. However, footnotes are used on occasion to assist readers exploring the topic further.

By the end of this book, you will have engaged numerous claims against the Bible. These claims will be dismantled by credible sources, textual evidence, and plain reason. As these claims against the Bible fall away one by one, your confidence in the life-giving, peace-bringing, sinner-saving ministry of Jesus Christ will be strengthened.

1

A BODY OF EVIDENCE

Why can I trust the Bible? Answer: Jesus.

Seriously, it is that simple. You do not need flowcharts and formulas to figure this out. Algorithms and syllogisms are not needed to prove that the Bible is trustworthy. There is no need for complication, consternation, or confusion: Jesus is why you can trust the Bible. The life, death, and resurrection of Jesus is the foundation for all trust in the Bible. This is simple. This is profound.

Get ready for some puzzling, perplexing, and profound discussions. This book will soon move beyond one-word answers. This book will get more complicated. You will learn all kinds of fancy words that you can use to impress your friends and sound smarter than you really are: *homologoumena, antilegomena, lectio difficilior,* and *lectio brevior.* (There is a glossary on p. 228 for reference.) You will engage in discussions about mythology, textual criticism, and world religions. The arguments for trusting the Bible will gain depth and complexity, and you will be intellectually stretched.

Still, the most basic reason for trusting the Bible is profoundly simple: Jesus. He is the reason God spoke through the Bible in the first place. He is the purpose of Scripture, the point of it all, and the primary source of its authority. The influence of Jesus is felt through all Scripture. He is anticipated in the Old Testament, experienced in the

Gospels, and evoked in the rest of the New Testament. If God had not come to redeem His creation in the flesh-and-blood person of Jesus, then there would be no need for the Bible. If Jesus did not truly live in human history with a fully human body, then the Bible would just be another good book about some fictional character. If God did not raise Jesus from the dead, then the Bible would be nothing more than a history book. Take Jesus out of the Bible, and there is nothing left.

The good news is He lives. Jesus lived, died, and now lives again. The earliest followers of Jesus referred to this as *evangelion,* which translates into "good news." The Bible is good news. To be certain, news is not a piece of advice or one person's opinion. It is not spiritual speculation or murky mysticism. News is about something that actually happened. The Bible is not a dusty book full of outdated advice; it is a life-changing book centered on the good news that God has acted in human history through Jesus Christ. The living Jesus greets us at the beginning of the Bible. He proclaims His return at the end of the Bible. And He speaks to us with every word in between. Scripture is dripping with Jesus.

Jesus precedes, predates, and presides over Scripture. He existed before the Bible. Indeed, the incarnation of Jesus occurred after the writing of the Old Testament. He was physically born after the Old Testament writings of Moses and Malachi, Jeremiah and Jonah. Nevertheless, Jesus existed in eternity before the incarnation. He was there in the beginning when the earth was without form and void. God spoke creation into existence through Him. Before there was a Bible, there was Jesus.

And Jesus would still exist even if the Bible ceased to exist. Imagine that every Bible in the world disappeared. Suppose that every shred of Scripture went away. Visualize that every Bible app on every smartphone and tablet crashed. Think the unthinkable: what if the Bible ceased to exist? If the Bible ceased to be, there would still be Jesus. He is the Word made flesh. His flesh-and-blood existence does not depend on the Bible; the Bible depends on His flesh-and-blood existence. The Bible does not validate Jesus; Jesus validates the Bible. The existence of the Bible is not the foundation for the existence of Jesus; the existence of Jesus is the foundation for the existence of the Bible. Trust in Jesus is not based on trust in the Bible; trust in the Bible is based on trust in Jesus. Jesus is the real and living person around whom the Bible coheres.

RESURRECTION PROOF

This sounds great. Yet, there is one nagging question that should be giving you a headache right now: if trust in the Bible is based on trust in Jesus, then how can I trust in Jesus without first trusting in the Bible? How could I possibly know anything about Jesus apart from the Bible? Everything I know about Jesus has come from the Gospels, right?

Access to Jesus is largely mediated through the Bible. The Old Testament provides prophecies pointing to the coming of Jesus. The Gospels tell us what He did and said. The New Testament explains how communities of people lived in the new life of Jesus. Is there anything about Jesus that exists apart from the Bible?

Yes. The resurrected body of Jesus exists today apart from the Bible. He lived. He died. And He lives today with a physically resurrected body. Jesus is literally the body of evidence around which the Scriptures cohere. Even if the Bible ceased to exist, the risen body of Jesus would still exist. The resurrected body of Jesus is why you can trust the Bible. You know that Jesus was raised from the dead not only because the Bible reports it but also because real people witnessed His really resurrected body with their own eyes.

Real people—Mary Magdalene, Peter, Thomas, Cleopas, Paul, and hundreds of others—had ocular proof of the resurrected Jesus. Mary had a real conversation with the really resurrected Jesus. Thomas physically touched the physically resurrected body of Jesus. The disciples witnessed Jesus as He consumed a fish and digested it with His resurrected organs. Paul had a bone-jarring, briefly blinding experience when he witnessed the risen Jesus. These are real people with real bodies who witnessed the real resurrected Jesus.

"But I haven't seen His body. . . . " That is true. Others witnessed the resurrected Jesus and told you about it. Take a moment and think about what else you trust in that you have not actually seen with your own eyes. Did you actually witness the assassination of Abraham Lincoln? Were you there when John Hancock signed the Declaration of Independence? Have you touched the iceberg that sunk the *Titanic*? Have you actually met Napoleon Bonaparte, Joan of Arc, or Alexander the Great? Nevertheless, there is little doubt that these events actually occurred or these people actually existed. Other people witnessed these events and met these individuals. These eyewitnesses then passed along their testimony to later generations.

Similarly, trust in the resurrection of Jesus is based on eyewitness accounts. There is literally a body of evidence arguing that the Bible is trustworthy. That body of evidence goes by the name *Jesus*. The resurrected body of Jesus proves that God does more than just speak into human history; He has definitively acted in human history through the resurrection of Jesus. God works through words and actions. He does not speak without action. He does not act without speaking. God speaks and acts, declares and delivers. The Bible is inextricably linked with the resurrection of Jesus.

When people witnessed this body of evidence—the living, breathing, and fully alive body of Jesus—they told others. These eyewitness accounts went viral. They were passed down from generation to generation. News about the resurrection traveled through many different communication channels:

Verbal Testimony. Before everything else, there was the spoken word. The spoken word—"Christ is risen!"—predates the Gospels, Epistles, and creedal confessions. This rich oral tradition of storytelling, preaching, and conversation quickly circulated the news of the living Jesus. Before the events of Jesus' life were organized into a creed and written down, there were eyewitnesses telling their own stories of seeing the risen Jesus.

Creeds. These are short statements of belief spoken in early Christian communities. Before the writings of the New Testament, they provided a way for news of the resurrection to be passed down from eyewitnesses to later generations. These brief confessions were easily remembered and used to help teach new followers of Jesus. Many of the early creeds made their way into various parts of the New Testament. Later creeds include the Apostles' Creed, the Nicene Creed, and the Athanasian Creed.

New Testament. The books of the New Testament are certainly the most familiar way the good news of Jesus is passed down from generation to generation. Each of the Gospels provides detailed accounts of the death and resurrection of Jesus. These historical accounts, along with numerous letters circulating from church to church, provided a way for people to hear about the resurrection of Jesus. This form of communication, however, did not arise immediately. It was at least a decade after the resurrection before the first New Testament writings appeared.

The Bible itself references all these ways in which the good news of the resurrection went viral. For example, the apostle Paul relies on all three of these communication channels as he writes to the Corinthians:

> For I delivered to you as of first importance what I also received: that Christ died for our sins in accordance with the Scriptures, that He was buried, that He was raised on the third day in accordance with the Scriptures, and that He appeared to Cephas, then to the twelve. Then

He appeared to more than five hundred brothers at one time, most of whom are still alive, though some have fallen asleep. Then He appeared to James, then to all the apostles. Last of all, as to one untimely born, He appeared also to me. (1 Corinthians 15:3–8)

Many biblical scholars believe that verses 3–7 of this text are a quotation from an early Christian creed. It appears that these words echo a creed confessed by many other Christian communities. Notice the references to Scripture and eyewitness testimony in this creedal confession about the resurrection of Jesus. These historical events in the life of Jesus—His death and resurrection—happened in accordance with the Scriptures. Since the New Testament did not yet exist, this is a reference to the books of the Old Testament. The historical events of Jesus' life lined up with the prophetic words of Scripture. Along with Scripture, this creed references the eyewitness testimony surrounding the resurrection. Eyewitnesses saw the body of evidence and told others of the resurrection of Jesus. Before you can discredit these words, you have to discredit every witness to the resurrection: Cephas, the Twelve, the five hundred, James, all the apostles, and Paul.

The Bible can be trusted because there is a body of evidence.

The point is simple: the Bible can be trusted because there is a body of evidence. That body of evidence is the living, breathing, fully resurrected body of Jesus. People saw it. People touched it. People were frightened by it. God has worked in human history through the flesh and blood person of Jesus, who was victorious over death. This historical event was promised in the Old Testament, proclaimed in the Gospels, and pervades the rest of the New Testament. God not only has spoken in history through the Bible, but He also has worked in human history through the death and resurrection of Jesus. God's speaking in the Bible is proved worthy of trust by God's working in human history.

RESURRECTION DIFFERENCE

The resurrection of Jesus is the body of evidence proving that the Bible is trustworthy. The historical life, death, and resurrection of Jesus is the defining feature separating the Bible from any other religious text. The living person of Jesus separates the Bible from every other holy book in history and around the globe. Without the resurrection of Jesus, the Bible would be no different from the Book of Mormon of the Latter-day Saints or the Qur'an of Muslims.

Other religious texts claim to be filled with divine words carrying divine authority. Trust in religious texts can come from one of two places: internal and external. Many religious texts make internal truth claims; they elicit the trust of readers by simply declaring they are true, infallible, and authoritative. They boldly proclaim that they are divine words free from error and full of power. They claim they should be trusted because they have claimed that they should be trusted. These holy books say they are trustworthy because they are holy books. The circular reasoning of these texts can be dizzying.

Trust in the Bible arises both internally and externally. Like other religious texts, the Bible declares itself to be true, infallible, and authoritative: "All Scripture is breathed out by God and profitable for teaching, for reproof, for correction, and for training in righteousness, that the man of God may be complete, equipped for every good work" (2 Timothy 3:16–17). However, unlike other religious texts, the Bible does not rely only on internal claims of trustworthiness. The resurrection of Jesus is the defining external feature separating the Bible from any other religious text. His death and resurrection is the supreme external source of trust for the Bible. Every word, teaching, and promise in the Bible can be trusted not only because the Bible claims it can be trusted, but also because it was confirmed outside the Bible in human history by the resurrection of Jesus. The Bible claims internally that it can be trusted and it is externally shown to be trustworthy by the resurrection of Jesus.

For example, suppose you are in a bookstore browsing through various books. You stop for a moment and look closely at personal finance books. The first book you pick up discusses how to get out of debt, increase savings, and profitably invest your money. The author offers no external reason, evidence, or experience as to why her methods work; she simply repeats throughout the chapters that her methods can be trusted and that you should be putting her methods into practice. You rightfully set the book down. The next book you pick up is also about personal finance. However, this one is full of external reasons, evidence, and experiences resulting in trustworthy methods. This author constantly repeats that her methods can be trusted because they are the result of real experiences. She invites you to trust not only her but also the real lives that have been changed by these methods. Which book do you want to buy?

Neglecting the historical event of the resurrection sets the Bible on the same plane as every other religious text. Without the life, death, and resurrection of Jesus, the Bible is just like every other book that claims to be trustworthy. With the life, death, and resurrection of Jesus, there is a body of evidence witnessed by hundreds of people proclaiming that the Bible can be trusted.

WHAT YOU NEED TO KNOW

Why can you trust the Bible? Jesus. The perennial Sunday School answer is actually right. Jesus is the central source of trust in the Bible. His life, death, and resurrection are historical events that happened in time and space. The resurrection of Jesus was witnessed by hundreds of people. Many of those eyewitnesses were full of skepticism and doubt. Thomas clearly had reservations about the possibility of a dead man coming back to life. Paul disbelieved the resurrection of Jesus so strongly that he was willing to persecute those who did believe. Nevertheless, Thomas and Paul became witnesses of the living and breathing Jesus who was victorious over death. These two witnesses—and hundreds of others—experienced the risen Jesus. This good news simultaneously confirmed the Old Testament and laid the foundation for the New Testament.

Why can you trust the Bible? Jesus.

The Bible is centered on the life, death, and resurrection of Jesus. He is why you can trust the Bible. The Scriptures cohere around this external, historical event witnessed by many. The resurrected Jesus is a living, breathing body of evidence validating the Bible. He is the cornerstone of the Christian faith. And He is the cornerstone of the Bible.

STUDY QUESTIONS

CHAPTER 1

1. Why is it important that Jesus is the foundation for trust in the Bible?

2. Who were some eyewitnesses of the resurrection of Jesus?

3. Eyewitness testimony was trusted in the ancient world. Do people still rely on the account of an eyewitness today?

4. Are there other instances in Scripture besides the resurrection where eyewitness accounts are relied upon?

5. There are numerous creeds in the Bible. Some examples include Deuteronomy 6:4 and Romans 10:9. Why were creedal confessions so important in the ancient world? Why are creedal confessions still important today?

6. Why is the resurrection of Jesus included in all of the Gospels while other events are included in only a few of the Gospels?

7. Why is external evidence important for establishing trust in the Bible?

2

MYTHS AND MIXTURES

In the beginning was the nothingness of Chaos. Gaia arose from this nothingness as the mother of all, the oldest one, and the foundation of all life. She was Mother Earth, giving life to all the earth. She gave birth to lesser gods. These demigods gave life to others. And this is how life began.

In the beginning was a tremendous explosion. The universe arose from this single big bang. All matter and energy in space, including the earth and all stars, were formed in this one moment. Living creatures then evolved over many billions of years through a process of mutation, random selection, and survival of the fittest. And this is how life began.

In the beginning was God. He spoke and created all things. The earth and the universe, land and water, animals and humans came from God's creative work over six days. On the seventh day, God reflected on His creation, declared it very good, and rested. And this is how life began.

In the beginning was the Flying Spaghetti Monster. This deity impulsively formed the earth in a state of inebriation. Since he had accidentally created all that is in existence, the earth lacked order, structure, and design. This noodly creator created a world that was deeply flawed, erratic, and incomprehensible. And this is how life began.

We have a problem.

You just read four creation accounts. They are explanations for the origin of the universe and all life therein. All of these accounts claim to be trustworthy depictions of the origin of the universe; each assumes to be the authoritative and accurate depiction of how life began. These depictions of the beginning do not leave room for other depictions; each account demands that all the others are false. And this is exactly the problem: conflicting accounts about the origin of the universe cannot all be trustworthy. One must be trustworthy and the others must not be trustworthy. One must be true and the others must be false. One must accurately convey the origins of life and the others must be myths.

Many have tried to place the Bible in the "myth" category. Scholars and skeptics have dismissed depictions of the creation, the flood, and the miracles and resurrection of Jesus as mythological tales. They have claimed that the Bible is as trustworthy as the ancient Greek depiction of Gaia or the modern depiction of the Flying Spaghetti Monster. (By the way, the Flying Spaghetti Monster is not something that I made up for this book; it is a religious parody that a large following of people claim to be true.) They have argued that the evolutionary account is fact and anything else is fable. The entire contents of the Bible have been stamped with permanent ink: MYTH.

The Bible is not a collection of mythological musings or mistaken miracles.

The Bible is not a collection of mythological musings or mistaken miracles. It is a historically accurate depiction of God's work in creation. It is the Word of God spoken with divine authority and authenticity. It is the only accurate depiction of reality. It surpasses the ancient Greek account of Gaia, the modern scientific account of Darwinian macroevolution, and the satirical account of the Flying Spaghetti Monster. Far from a mythological story, every page of the biblical account is trustworthy.

CLAIM:

THE BIBLE IS MERELY A MYTHOLOGICAL STORY SIMILAR TO HOMER'S *ODYSSEY.*

Ignorance abounds in this claim. Any person making this argument proves only one point: he or she knows nothing about the study of mythology, the Bible, or Homer's *Odyssey*. Rather than breaking trust in the Bible, this argument breaks trust in the one making the claim.

The simple response is that the Bible is not a mythological story. It may share certain similarities to mythological texts; however, that does not mean the Bible is a mythological text. Jesus did not approach the Bible as mythology. He memorized, prayed, and espoused the Scriptures. Jesus spoke of Adam, Eve, Moses, Jonah, and David as historic people. The disciples and those in the Early Church knew that it was not mythology; nobody dies the horrific death of a martyr for a myth. Subsequent recipients of the Bible did not approach it as a myth. There is absolutely no basis for modern readers to deem the Bible a mere mythological tale.

A more complex response is a bit more nuanced. Before you can see what makes the Bible more than a fanciful story, you need to know something about the study of mythology. People often assume that a myth is nothing more than a fabricated story. They reduce all mythology down to one determining factor: is it true? If an account is true, then it is not a myth. If an account is not true, then it is a myth.

This is an antiquated and oversimplified understanding of mythology; however, it was the accepted view of mythology at one time. Many scholars during the nineteenth century dismissed ancient religious texts as unsophisticated, inaccurate, and historically flawed.

These scholars assumed that all ancient accounts depicting creation, floods, or heroic figures were simply prescientific and premodern attempts to interpret the natural world. They classified ancient religious texts as dubious accounts of history. They stamped them all MYTH: false, fictional, and fabricated.

Modern scholars have taken quite a different approach to ancient texts depicting creation, floods, and heroic figures. Rather than directly dismissing these texts as false, modern scholars now seek to discover how myths function in establishing models of behavior, reenacting a past event, and making sense of profound mystery. Rather than overlooking myths as historically inaccurate, modern scholars study how they functioned within a culture. Modern scholars of mythology are far less interested in determining the text true or false. Rather, they study how the text worked to shape the culture.

There is no denying that the Bible has some similarities with mythical texts. The Bible helps make sense of God's will and work in creation just as the Egyptian texts depicting the concept of Ma'at tried to make sense of social order and justice. Scripture brings past events into the present just as Roman citizens used to tell the myth of Rome's founding to explain its magnificence. Scripture shapes how we live our lives just as the tale of Icarus trying to fly toward the sun shaped people's values in the Greco-Roman culture. Nevertheless, simply because the Bible shares similarities with mythological texts does not mean it is a myth. History books on the British monarchy share certain similarities to Shakespeare's *King Richard III*, yet this does not mean that these history books ought to be classified as drama. Scripture can share similarities with mythological texts yet not be a myth.

The Bible is not a mythological text. There is no justification for placing Scripture in the same category as Virgil's *Aeneid*, Homer's *Odyssey*, or the *Epic of Gilgamesh*. Unlike these texts, the Bible is historically accurate, confirmed by extrabiblical accounts, and verified by archaeologists. Unlike Atlas, Apollo, or Artemis, Jesus of Nazareth is a historical person. He was born in Bethlehem, raised in Nazareth, and died on a cross at Golgotha. No reputable historian would argue *for* the existence of Atlas just as no reputable historian would argue *against* the existence of Jesus of Nazareth. Unlike mythological figures, Jesus lived in real places that testify to His real existence. Unlike the mythical founding of Rome, there is actual archaeological evidence for the Israelites in the Promised Land. Archaeologists have discovered proof that the biblical account is historically accurate. The response to this claim is clear and simple: the Bible is not a mythological text.

THE BIBLE > MYTHOLOGY

The Bible is greater than mythology. It is the Word of God. It is holy, eternal, powerful, authoritative, and life-giving. Every word in the Bible is dripping with holiness because God cannot speak anything but holy words. Every word in Scripture is timeless and eternal because God is without beginning or end and His Word is never obsolete. The Bible has the power to change heaven and hell, earth and everything in between. God's powerful Word created the universe, commandeers wayward sinners, and comforts broken souls. Scripture exceeds all other texts in authority. God has the final word on truth, wisdom, justice, beauty, and life.

God's Word—unlike the words of Aesop, Homer, and Virgil—is timeless and eternal: "The grass withers, the flower fades, but the word of our God will stand forever" (Isaiah 40:8). Other ancient texts are nothing more than a faint echo through the corridors of history, whereas God is still triumphantly heralding His promises in Scripture. Alive with God's power, the Bible is far from the dusty, dead, and decrepit words of mythology: "For the word of God is living and active, sharper than any two-edged sword, piercing to the division of soul and of spirit, of joints and of marrow, and discerning the thoughts and intentions of the heart" (Hebrews 4:12). It bears repeating: the Bible is God's Word—holy, eternal, powerful, authoritative, and life-giving.

This does not mean that the Bible descended from heaven pre-bound, untouched by human hands, and ready for the Church to read. Despite being the very Word of God, human authors composed the books of the Bible. God's Word has human fingerprints all over it. And nobody is trying to hide that fact. There are numerous examples of its human authorship: "I, Paul, write this greeting with my own hand. This is the sign of genuineness in every letter of mine; it is the way I write" (2 Thessalonians 3:17). There are even examples of the human authors of Scripture expressing their human concerns: "The churches of Asia send you greetings. Aquila and Prisca, together with the church in their house, send you hearty greetings in the Lord. All the brothers send you greetings. Greet one another with a holy kiss. I, Paul, write this greeting with my own hand" (1 Corinthians 16:19–21).

Human authorship does not exclude divine authorship. God composed the books of the Bible through human authors. Moses, David, Paul, John, and all the others were used by God to compose His Holy Word. Just as it is accurate to discuss Moses' word in Deuteronomy, David's word in the Psalms, or Paul's word in Corinthians; it is also accurate to discuss God's Word in Deuteronomy, God's Word in the Psalms, and God's Word in Corinthians. Both are correct depictions of Scripture. God's Word mediated through human words is nothing new: God put words in Moses' and Aaron's mouths in order to confront Pharaoh (Exodus 4:10–17). God spoke through the human mouths of the prophets such as Jeremiah, Jonah, and Joel. God used human words written on the wall to condemn the reign of Belshazzar (Daniel 5). God spoke eternal life through Peter's proclamation of the Gospel at Pentecost (Acts 2:14–41). The Holy Spirit uses human mouths to proclaim the Word of God. This is not scandalous. This is the wonderful mystery of God's work in creation.

And Jesus shows how God is willing to speak words through human flesh. God came in human flesh in the person of Jesus Christ. Jesus is God in human flesh. He is the divine Word made flesh: "The Word became flesh and dwelt among us, and we have seen His glory, glory as of the only Son from the Father, full of grace and truth" (John 1:14). God is not afraid of using His creation—flesh and blood, nails and wood, words and writing, text and alphabet, paper and books—to perform His work of salvation.

This means that the Bible is both eternal and historic. It is timeless, boundless, permanent, and transcendent. And it was written in a particular language using particular expressions, idioms, and sayings. The Holy Spirit enlightens believers to comprehend and cling to the words of Scripture. And human diligence, learning, and study are employed in order to engage the Bible with understanding. The Bible is practical and applicable to all people. And it was written to a specific people in a specific location. These tensions are unique to Scripture. Since the Bible is unlike any other text in human history, it is not at all surprising that it has its own unique tensions, challenges, and idiosyncrasies.

WHAT YOU NEED TO KNOW

The Bible is greater than any mythological text. It did not shape just the lives of people living thousands of years ago. It continues to shape the lives of people today. The Bible is not just the words of human authors like the work of Homer or Aesop. It is the true and powerful Word of God composed through human authors. The Bible is not about fictitious people with no historical context. It is about real people living in real history. The Bible is no mythological text. It is something far greater: God's Word.

CLAIM:

THERE ARE MANY OTHER CREATION STORIES BEYOND THE BIBLICAL ACCOUNT IN GENESIS. THE VERSION IN GENESIS IS JUST ONE OF THE MANY OTHER FICTITIOUS STORIES.

This claim is really troubling . . . until you stop to think about it. Some questions and curiosities are innately human: Who am I? Where did I come from? Where did the world come from? These are questions that all people in all places at all times have asked. They are not unique to any one time or culture. Humans ask these sorts of questions in order to gain self-understanding. It is no surprise, then, that every culture throughout history would have an account of human origins. Asking questions of origin, known as cosmology, is a natural human impulse. This is like walking into your kitchen and finding a plate of freshly made cookies. The obvious question is "Who made this wonderful surprise?" In other words, where did these cookies come from? And then, usually before your question is answered, you eat them.

Cosmological questions are innately human. The desire to know the origin of the earth and life is deep within our bones. This is a question that consumes scientists and theologians, scholars and bus drivers, children and adults. It is no surprise that there have been many different creation stories told throughout human history. This chapter began with a few of the most commonly known, nonbiblical accounts:

Gaia: Greek mythology is the source of the story of Gaia, the creator and giver of life to the earth and the universe. According to this myth, Gaia gave birth to all things and is the mother of the earth. Her union with Uranus led to the heavenly gods, the Titans, and the Giants. Modern depictions of Mother Nature and Mother Earth draw heavily on the creation account of Gaia.

Big Bang Theory: Scientists are responsible for the account known as the big bang theory, which states that the birth of the universe happened roughly thirteen billion years ago when an extremely dense and hot state expanded and cooled. This initial trajectory continues today as the universe is still expanding. This origin account was developed in the twentieth century, yet widely accepted only in the latter part of the century. Although not all scientists assume this creatorless cosmology when doing scientific research, many do hold to it.

Flying Spaghetti Monster: This parody account of the earth's origin came as a result of a school-board debate regarding science curriculum. It began as an open letter asking that the Church of the Flying Spaghetti Monster's cosmology be taught in schools. Although it is obviously a satirical account, Flying Spaghetti Monster (FSM) symbols adorn clothing, car bumpers, and coffee cups.

These creation stories, along with thousands of others, all agree on one point: the world came from somewhere. There must be an explanation for the origin of life. It is neither surprising nor scandalous that there are multiple creation stories in existence. The trouble comes with all the radical differences between the various accounts. Some rely on God or gods while others rely on inanimate forces and physics. Some depict a creation that is ordered and very good while others depict the creation as chaotic and incomplete. These discrepancies are a problem: which creation account is accurate? Is the Genesis account simply one of many thousands of ancient stories trying to explain the origin of the earth and life?

There is an excess of evidence suggesting that the Genesis creation account is authoritative. When all the evidence is viewed together, it is obvious that the origin of the earth depicted in Genesis is credible.

Jesus: The importance of Jesus treating the Book of Genesis as authoritative cannot be overemphasized. He affirmed God as creator (Mark 13:19) and recognized that Adam and Eve were real people in God's creation (Mark 10:6). Jesus further upheld a six-day creation when He affirmed the Old Testament teaching that God created for six days and then rested on the Sabbath (Mark 2:23–28). Jesus did not treat Genesis as false or fictitious, poetic or passé. He never suggested that Genesis was an option among many other equally valid options. Jesus depicted Genesis as the authoritative creation account over the panoply of other creation stories. He taught from it with boldness and confidence. And Genesis mentions Jesus when God proclaims after sin enters creation, "I will put enmity between you and the woman, and between your offspring and her offspring; He shall bruise your head, and you shall bruise His heel" (Genesis 3:15). The triumphant Offspring promised in Genesis is Jesus.

Science: Yes, you read that correctly. Science provides evidence that the Genesis creation account is accurate. One of the most fundamental assumptions of science is consistency. Science relies on consistency in the causes that operate in the natural world: objects in motion will consistently remain in motion unless acted on by an external force; H_2O in a gaseous state consistently has more energy than H_2O in a solid state. There is no happenstance or random selection in the creation account of Genesis; rather, it depicts a creation that is intelligently designed, ordered, consistent, and predictable. Other creation stories—the ancient Greek account filled with quarreling gods and goddesses, the Babylonian account of competing creators, and the Iroquois account of mud piled atop a floating turtle—lack the constancy required for scientific inquiry. Countless discoveries ranging from astronomy to zoology have come from scientists holding to the creation account in Genesis. Today, many scientists continue to do research from a Genesis-based, intelligent-design paradigm.

History: Human history confirms that Genesis is trustworthy. The Genesis account is deemed authoritative by what has occurred in subsequent generations. Abraham received a bold promise in Genesis: "Abram fell on his face. And God said to him, 'Behold, My covenant is with you, and you shall be the father of a multitude of nations. No longer shall your name be called Abram, but your name shall be Abraham, for I have made you the father of a multitude of nations. I will make you exceedingly fruitful, and I will make you into nations, and kings shall come from you'" (Genesis 17:3–6). This promise has been confirmed in human history by the Abrahamic faiths (Christianity, Judaism, and Islam) tracing their lineage back to Abraham. Over half of the world's population identifies with one of the three Abrahamic religions. Absolutely no other ancient text has this sort of historical confirmation.

There is nothing scandalous about the existence of other creation accounts beyond what is recorded in Genesis. The cornucopia of creation stories known to historians is easily explained by events recorded in the Bible. The dispersion of tribes and nations is depicted in Genesis: "These are the generations of the sons of Noah, Shem, Ham, and Japheth. Sons were born to them after the flood" (10:1). From these three sons, tribes and nations formed and spread throughout the world. "From these the coastland peoples spread in their lands, each with his own language, by their clans, in their nations" (10:5). The story of creation as told in Genesis was then told, retold, and untold in many different ways. From the trustworthy account in Genesis came countless other accounts, each varying in accuracy and reliability. Just as a family story retold by later generations shifts and shapes anew, the story of creation in Genesis changed as it spread throughout nations and lands.

WHAT YOU NEED TO KNOW

Genesis is certainly not the only creation account. There are thousands of others. Nevertheless, the creation account in Genesis is the only one confirmed by Jesus as trustworthy, corroborated by generations of scientific inquiry, and confirmed by history. It is no myth. It is not magic. It offers no misinformation. It is trustworthy.

CLAIM:

NUMEROUS FLOOD STORIES EXIST FROM ANTIQUITY. THE BIBLICAL STORY OF NOAH AND THE ARK IS A MIXTURE OF FLOOD STORIES FROM OTHER CULTURES.

The existence of other flood accounts is no surprise. In fact, the existence of other flood accounts is a relief, because it further proves that a catastrophic, history-altering flood actually happened. These other flood accounts just add more credence to the biblical flood in Genesis 6–9. There would be reason for skepticism if a geologically unprecedented flood happened and nobody else in human history ever made mention of it.

There are well over a hundred prehistoric deluge stories in existence today. Some scholars estimate that the number of ancient flood stories is closer to three hundred. These descriptions of an ancient flood are both culturally and geographically diverse. Many of these flood stories have come from ancient peoples in Mesopotamia, the Americas, and Asia. Still others have been discovered in Europe, Africa, Australia, and the South Sea Islands. It is apparent from all these accounts that the historical memory of a cataclysmic flood was commonplace.

Nearly all of the ancient flood accounts contain three main features:

1. humankind and animals are universally destroyed by water;

2. a boat of some kind provides respite; and

3. a seed of mankind is preserved to continue the human race.

Unlike a creation story, a catastrophic flood story is not necessary for a person's self-understanding. Tribes and nations do not need to have a flood story to explain their history. This further proves that the flood was a historical reality; it is illogical to think that over a hundred ancient societies concocted a flood story simply because it was entertaining. Something must have happened.

The account of Noah as depicted in Genesis came out of the ancient Near East. There exist three other popular deluge accounts from this time and place. Their relatively similar place and time of origin raises questions: Are they three different versions of one fictional story? Are they different interpretations of an actual prehistoric cataclysmic flood? Or are they some combination of fiction and reality?

The *Eridu* Genesis account is traditionally dated to late in the Old Babylonian period (circa 1600 BC). The manuscript is found on a Sumerian tablet of which only the lower third is preserved. The section of the text that scholars possess begins with humanity becoming civilized and creating too much noise so as to prompt a flood by the gods. The king, Ziusudra, is warned and preserved by means of a boat. However, missing portions of the narration make it impossible to know beyond conjecture who else was spared besides King Ziusudra.

Another ancient Near Eastern flood story is the *Atrahasis Epic*. This text was composed sometime in the first half of the second millennium BC.[1] This account begins with lower deities who are sick of their work and thus create humans to work in their stead. The humans continue to grow in number and later become too noisy, so the gods send a plague, a famine, and finally a drought to deplete the human population. Since these attempts remain unsuccessful, the gods send a flood. Atrahasis is warned about the impending destruction

---

1   W. G. Lambert, A. R. Millard, and Miguel Civil, eds. *Atra-hasis: The Babylonian Story of the Flood.* (Oxford: Oxford University Press, 1969).

and resolves to build a boat in which animals, birds, and a portion of humanity is preserved.

The *Epic of Gilgamesh* is another one of the ancient Near Eastern deluge accounts. This epic is well-known by scholars. It is believed to be a compilation of multiple Mesopotamian works rather than an isolated piece of writing. The *Epic of Gilgamesh* is composed of twelve different tablets that recount Gilgamesh's search for immortality. Scholars typically place the *Epic of Gilgamesh* as originating somewhere around the Old Babylonian Period (2000–1600 BC), and it is thought to have circulated extensively during the Middle Babylonian Period (1600–1000 BC). The eleventh tablet of the epic tells the story of how Gilgamesh heard that a god named Utnapishtim had been a mortal human before he received immortality from the other gods. Gilgamesh asked Utnapishtim how he became a god. This prompted Utnapishtim to tell the story of the flood and subsequent gift of immortality. The excursus at the end of this chapter will provide a detailed analysis of this text.

THE BIBLE > ANCIENT EPICS

These three additional flood stories originated around the same time and place as the story of Noah in Genesis. Is it possible that one is right and the rest are wrong? What makes the Genesis account more authoritative than the other three? There are a number of reasons why the flood story in Genesis holds water. (That was a lame attempt at flood humor.)

> **Jesus:** Just as He confirmed the creation account in Genesis, Jesus also confirmed that the account of Noah is trustworthy. From His mouth came validation that the flood as depicted in Genesis is reliable: "They were eating and drinking and marrying and being given in marriage, until the day when Noah entered the ark, and the flood came and destroyed them all" (Luke 17:27). Jesus made it clear

that the biblical depiction of the flood—and none of the others—is the authoritative account. There is a counterargument that can be made to this: Jesus was Jewish and it only makes sense that He would turn to Genesis. He was raised on the Scriptures in the Old Testament and not the *Epic of Gilgamesh*. Nevertheless, this line of argumentation overlooks one crucial confession of Jesus: He is God. As God in human flesh, Jesus demonstrated that He was not restricted by the limitations of mere human knowledge (Mark 2:6–8; 11:2; John 1:48–49). If Jesus knew the hidden recesses of hearts and minds, then Jesus also knew about the *Epic of Gilgamesh*.

Genre: Scholars have classified all of the other Mesopotamian flood accounts as poetry. It is clear that the Atrahasis Epic and the *Epic of Gilgamesh* are epic poems. The Eridu Genesis, while not an epic, is clearly a form of Sumerian poetry. Ancient Near Eastern poetry and epics often depicted a heroic figure in highly figurative and imaginative language. Rather than citing specific facts and figures, these texts would sing refrains and offer vivid imagery: "The deluge bellowed like a bull, The wind resounded like a screaming eagle. The darkness was dense, the sun was gone" (Atrahasis Epic III.15). Unlike epic poetry, Genesis depicts a historical account of the flood: "And rain fell upon the earth forty days and forty nights. On the very same day Noah and his sons, Shem and Ham and Japheth, and Noah's wife and the three wives of his sons with them entered the ark" (7:12–13). The Genesis account is not a poetic recollection of a flood; rather, it is a historical narrative depicting real events in detail.

Plausibility: Genesis offers a more plausible account than the other Mesopotamian flood stories. The *Epic of Gilgamesh* depicts a cube-shaped boat made out of reeds. This boat was reportedly built in seven days. The cataclysmic flood came only from rain and lasted just seven days. Genesis reports a rectangular boat made out of wood and constructed over many years. The flood came from both rain and subterranean aquifers, and it took over a year before the land could be inhabited again (Genesis 7:6, 11; 8:13–14). The events recorded in Genesis are highly plausible. The events recorded in the epic flood poems simply do not float.

WHAT YOU NEED TO KNOW

There are numerous ancient flood stories. The abundance of these accounts confirms the reality of a cataclysmic flood in ancient times. Genesis contains the only flood account that Jesus confirmed as trustworthy. It is the only one to value historical accuracy over poetic invention. And it is the only one that is actually plausible.

The *Epic* of *Gilgamesh*

If you know just one ancient flood narrative, then it is most likely the depiction of Noah in Genesis. If you know two ancient flood narratives, then it is likely the depiction of Noah in Genesis and the *Epic of Gilgamesh*. Although there are more than a hundred ancient narratives recounting a cataclysmic flood, these two are by far the most widely known.

Scholars recognize the *Epic of Gilgamesh* as one of the most influential ancient texts. As stated earlier, it is composed of twelve different tablets that recount Gilgamesh's search for immortality. Tablet XI contains the epic's only reference to a cataclysmic flood. In this tablet, Gilgamesh hears about a god named Utnapishtim, who was a mortal human until he received immortality from the other gods. Gilgamesh asks Utnapishtim how this transpired, and the story of the flood and subsequent gift of immortality is recounted. Just as in Genesis, the epic's flood story interestingly also talks of birds that are sent to search for dry land and of a rainbow after the storm. This has led many people to speculate that the similarities

between the *Epic of Gilgamesh* and the account of the flood in Genesis are the result of literary borrowing.

Literary borrowing, the practice of taking one text and using it in another text, is sometimes used as a reason the Genesis account should not be trusted. According to this argument, the Genesis account of Noah and the flood is plagiarized from the *Epic of Gilgamesh*. Both texts originated in similar regions and share some striking similarities. Scholars suggest that as the Genesis text was being composed, someone had access to the *Epic of Gilgamesh* and thought it might make for a good addition. There are, however, some serious problems with this accusation of literary borrowing.

There are a number of sharp differences that distinguish the Genesis account from the *Epic of Gilgamesh*. God reveals the impending flood to Noah in the Genesis account: "And God said to Noah, 'I have determined to make an end of all flesh, for the earth is filled with violence through them. Behold, I will destroy them with the earth'" (6:13). Unlike God telling Noah about the flood and what he should do to escape it, the *Epic of Gilgamesh* depicts a series of secrets and lies: Utnapishtim secretly finds out about the impending flood from one of the gods (Ea) and then lies to everyone about why he is having them help build the boat. The shape of the boat is another difference in the accounts: Noah constructs a rectangular ark while Utnapishtim uses a square vessel. The source and length of the flood is substantially different between the two accounts: Genesis reports a flood consisting of both groundwater and rainwater (7:11), which lasted for forty days and forty nights (7:12), with the waters prevailing on the earth for one hundred and fifty days (7:24) and not abating for another several months (8:3–5). The Gilgamesh epic consists of only rainwater for no more than seven days.

Another massive difference between these flood narratives is that the Genesis story contains a monotheistic universe while the *Epic of Gilgamesh* contains a polytheistic cosmos that is full of conflicting gods. In the Genesis account, God is the sole determiner of the flood: "And God said to Noah, 'I have determined to make an end of all flesh'" (6:13). On the other hand, the divine pantheon determines the Gilgamesh flood. The council of gods decides to send the flood and then later regrets its decision. These two flood narratives depict fundamentally different realities.

Yet another difference between these two narratives is where the ark comes to rest. The *Epic of Gilgamesh* reports the location to be Mount Nisir, which is generally known as Pir Omar Gundrun in the region of Nuzi (modern-day Iraq). The Genesis account locates the final resting place of the ark on Mount Ararat (modern-day Turkey). This is a difference of nearly three hundred miles.

The differences in these two accounts clearly outweigh the similarities. There is simply no conclusive evidence that the Genesis account is the result of literary borrowing from the *Epic of Gilgamesh*. Since these accounts were originally shared through oral transmission, it is impossible to determine which one came first.

Nevertheless, it is undeniable that these two accounts are somehow related. Their geographic proximity and similarities suggest some sort of association. The explanation for their relationship is simple: a flood actually happened. Clearly a cataclysmic flood happened in human history and the survivors passed down the account to later generations. A real remnant of humanity was preserved in that flood. A real account of the event came off the boat after the waters receded. And that real account became corrupted as it was passed from generation to generation.

There is good evidence to suggest that the *Epic of Gilgamesh* is a corrupted account of the Genesis account. The primary evidence to support this claim is scientific—the Genesis account is plausible by scientific standards whereas the *Epic of Gilgamesh* is not. The material and structure of the vessel described in Genesis is architecturally superior to the reeds and square shape described in the *Epic of Gilgamesh*. The source of the water described in the biblical account is supported by modern hydrological knowledge. The length of the flood depicted in the Genesis account is scientifically plausible. The *Epic of Gilgamesh* simply cannot hold water when scrutinized by science. One can be trusted and the other cannot. The Genesis flood account is both historically and scientifically trustworthy. The *Epic of Gilgamesh* is not.

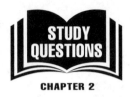

STUDY QUESTIONS

CHAPTER 2

1. What other creation accounts are you aware of? How do they depict the creation of the world?

2. What comes to mind when you hear the word *myth*?

3. The creation account in the Bible is not a fanciful myth. How does Scripture make it clear that it is not merely mythology?

4. God's Word is powerful. What are some ways that you have experienced the power of God's Word in your own life?

5. Read Genesis 6:11–22. Who is the central figure in this text?

6. Many other flood narratives depict a human as the central figure of the text. Why might these false narratives put humans at the center?

7. Why is it important to know of the existence of other ancient flood narratives?

3

ERRORS AND EDITS

Imagine that you are reading a textbook on American history. You open up the book and read the first page: "George Washington became President of the United States of America in 1791. He is remembered for his tremendous courage in leading the nation through it's war for independence. Washington's accomplishments show his tremendous attention to detale."

What do you think of this book so far? Is it reliable? Do you want to keep reading? You may notice that there are a few errors in the text. George Washington became president in 1789, not 1791. Strike one. The author uses "it's" rather than "its." Strike two. And the word *detail* is spelled incorrectly. Strike three.

Readers may allow one error in a text. Extremely patient readers might possibly continue reading after two errors. However, nearly all readers would close the book after encountering three errors. Mistakes, misspellings, and miscalculations discredit a text. Inaccuracies and inconsistencies leave readers distrusting and skeptical. Textual errors destroy textual authority.

Claims that the Bible is full of errors and edits are old. (Even older than the erroneous legend of George Washington cutting down a cherry tree.) Skeptics have been dismissing the Bible as error-filled and cleverly edited for centuries. And for centuries, these accusations have been disproven. The Bible is free from error. The Bible was not secretly edited behind closed doors. If anything is in error, it is the many claims made against the Bible.

CLAIM:

THE BIBLE HAS SO MANY TEXTUAL ERRORS THAT IT SIMPLY CANNOT BE TRUSTED.

This claim has so many errors of its own. Arguing that there are numerous "errors" in the Bible reveals a complete misunderstanding of the manuscript witnesses and textual variants. Asserting that the Bible cannot be trusted on account of the many errors suggests that the person making this claim has never taken the time to learn about how the Bible came into existence.

Understanding the process by which the Scriptures came into existence is vitally important to debunking this claim. Under the guidance of the Holy Spirit, the biblical authors recorded what God revealed to them. This divine revelation included insight into the mysteries of God and the meaning of His work in human history for salvation. These original texts written by the divinely inspired authors are called autographs. The autographs were copied and reproduced in order to share the writings with many people. The copies produced from the original autograph are known as manuscript witnesses. Therefore, there is only one autograph but many manuscript witnesses. Luke composed one Gospel of Luke (autograph) while scribes produced many copies of the Gospel of Luke (manuscript witnesses).

CAN I GET A (MANUSCRIPT) WITNESS?

Rather than coming from one single text, the biblical texts available to us today are composed of many, many manuscript copies. The Gospel of Luke that you read today, though composed by one person interviewing many eyewitnesses, is composed of many manuscript witnesses. These manuscript copies were not made on a photocopier, nor were the scribes able to take out their smartphones and snap a photo of the original text. Rather, the manuscript copies were composed by hand. Creating copies of a text in the ancient world was time-consuming and expensive; literate scribes were hard to come by, and the material needed was costly.

The Bible in your hand today is the result of thousands of manuscript witnesses discovered by archaeologists and scholars or preserved in ancient libraries and monasteries. These manuscript witnesses range from complete scrolls to fragments no bigger than your thumbnail. They range in age of composition and place of origin. Since there are large differences in historical period and language, it is helpful to discuss the Old Testament and New Testament manuscript witnesses separately.

OLD TESTAMENT MANUSCRIPTS

Although the Old Testament was composed thousands of years ago, many manuscript witnesses are still intact today. For generations, the oldest copies of the Old Testament writings were from the Septuagint. The Septuagint is a Greek translation of the Old Testament composed between 300–100 BC. The oldest copies of the Septuagint date back to roughly 200 BC. The oldest Hebrew version of the Old Testament was contained in the Aleppo Codex and the Leningrad Codex. These manuscripts date back to the tenth and eleventh centuries.

This all changed in 1947 with the discovery of the Dead Sea Scrolls in Qumran. A shepherd was searching for a wayward animal when he happened upon a cave. He threw a rock into the cave and he heard the sound of a clay pot shattering. He investigated the cave and found one of the greatest archaeological discoveries in human history. The discovery at Qumran revealed roughly nine hundred ancient manuscripts, many of which were copies of the Old Testament text written in Hebrew between 200 BC and AD 68. The discovery of the Dead Sea Scrolls pushed the date of the oldest Hebrew manuscripts back almost a thousand years. It is significant to note that although nearly a thousand years separated these two copies of the Old Testament, the differences between the manuscripts were insignificant. This refuted any claims that the biblical texts were changed or corrupted during this time. Over the course of a thousand years, the biblical text remained the same.

Over the course of a thousand years, the biblical text remained the same.

New Testament Manuscripts

There are significantly more New Testament manuscripts and fragments compared to the Old Testament. Much of this has to do with the culture and period of history in which these texts were written; the Greco-Roman world enjoyed widespread literacy and writing material. Roughly six thousand Greek New Testament manuscripts and fragments provide witness to the biblical text. More than nineteen thousand manuscripts and fragments written in other ancient languages (Latin, Syriac, Coptic, Armenian, etc.) provide further evidence. In other words, a total of twenty-five thousand ancient New Testament manuscripts have been discovered. This is significantly more than any other ancient text. For example, Homer's *Iliad* has only two-thousand manuscript witnesses.

In addition to being more numerous, the New Testament manuscripts are also significantly older than any other ancient text. The oldest manuscript witness—a portion of the Gospel of John known as P52—is dated back to AD 125. That means that less than two generations separate the autograph and the manuscript copy.

The oldest manuscript witnesses for classic works of literature such as Julius Caesar's *Gallic Wars* date back to only AD 900.[2]

The Bible—both the Old Testament and the New Testament—is composed of many manuscript witnesses. This wealth of evidence makes the biblical text trustworthy. Rather than drawing from one manuscript that is a thousand years older than the autograph, biblical scholars draw from thousands of manuscripts that are just a few generations older than the autograph.

UNDERSTANDING TEXTUAL VARIANTS

Thousands of manuscripts written across many different languages will certainly have differences. What happens when one manuscript disagrees with the others? Does it mean that the Bible is in error if two manuscript witnesses do not agree? Biblical scholars refer to these discrepancies in the manuscripts as textual variants. Here are some examples of the most common sorts of textual variants in the Bible:

> Matthew 1:6—Some manuscripts have "David," while other manuscripts have "David the king."
>
> Matthew 6:25—Some manuscripts have "**or** what you will drink," while other manuscripts have "**and** what you will drink."
>
> Luke 8:26—Some manuscripts have "Gerasenes," while others have "Gergesenes" or "Gadarenes."
>
> Psalm 22:16—Some manuscripts have "they have pierced my hands and feet," while others have "like a lion [they are at] my hands and feet."

While the vast majority of textual variants are minor syntactical discrepancies, there are also a few substantial variants in the manu-

---

2 F. F. Bruce, *The New Testament Documents: Are They Reliable?* (Downer's Grove: InterVarsity Press, 1964), 16.

script witnesses. These are the most noteworthy textual variants in the Bible:

> Mark 16:9–20—There are textual variants in the final chapter of the Gospel of Mark. Some manuscripts end at verse 8 while other manuscripts include verses 9–20. It should be noted that nothing in the longer version of Mark is troubling or scandalous in any way.

> John 7:53–8:11—The account of Jesus and the woman caught in adultery is not included in many manuscripts. This raises questions about why only some manuscripts include this event in the ministry of Jesus. As with Mark 16, this account does not substantially change the character or teachings of Jesus.

> 1 John 5:7–8—Later manuscripts include an explicit trinitarian reference: "the Father, the Word and the Holy Spirit." This sentence is not found in any Greek manuscript before the fourteenth century.

The vast majority of textual variants are insignificant and do not change the biblical narrative in any meaningful way.

Apart from a few exceptions, the vast majority of textual variants are insignificant and do not change the biblical narrative in any meaningful way. When variant readings are discovered in the manuscript witnesses, there is a well-established protocol for determining which reading is most accurate. This practice of establishing the best text is known as textual criticism. The aim of textual criticism is not necessarily to criticize or undermine the biblical text; however, some scholars have endeavored to destroy the authority of the Bible through textual criticism. Determining authorship, date, and quality of the manuscript witness are central aims of textual criticism.

Establishing the best text is not a matter of individual speculation. Textual criticism offers certain principles for determining which variant reading is most accurate to the original text:

Lectio difficilior potior: This is Latin for "the more difficult reading is stronger." This principle of textual criticism asserts that the more difficult reading is most likely closest to the original text. It seems backward that the more difficult reading would be prioritized over clearer readings. There is, however, a very good reason for this principle. As scribes and copyists produced manuscripts, they would often try to improve on the text. When sentences were unclear in any way, the person copying the text would add a word or change the sentence structure in order to render clearer readings. As manuscripts were copied and recopied, minor changes were made to improve the reading. Therefore, the more difficult readings are likely older and closer to the original text.

Lectio brevior: This is Latin for "shorter reading." This principle of textual criticism asserts that the shorter reading is most likely the closest to the original text. This principle is closely related to the previous one. As biblical texts were copied and recopied, scribes would add a word or phrase in order to help the reader better understand the sentence. This made the copied manuscripts slightly longer than the original manuscripts. Therefore, the shorter readings are considered the older readings and are therefore closer to the original text.

External Evidence: Certain external factors are important in determining the reliability of a manuscript witness. These factors include the date, source, and relationship to other witnesses. Older manuscripts are given priority over newer manuscripts since variants often accumulate over time. Texts copied by a skilled copyist, as evidenced by factors such as handwriting and other composition practices, are prioritized over manuscripts with numerous scribal errors.

Simply dismissing the Bible as full of errors is an error itself. This claim is an unreflective dismissal of thousands of manuscript witnesses. And it reveals a strong hypocrisy within the person making this claim. Suppose that a person dismisses the Bible on account of textual variants in the ancient manuscripts. This person would also have to dismiss every one of the classics from antiquity. And the works of Shakespeare. And the Gettysburg Address. And thousands of other respected texts.

The notion of a single text being identically reproduced hundreds of thousands of times is relatively new. Scanners, photocopiers, and computers (digital duplicators) are less than a century old. Before the invention of these digital duplicators, there were mechanical duplicators—such as printing presses, letter-copying presses, and mimeographs. These mechanical devices allowed for document duplication that was significantly faster than handwriting a copy. Nevertheless, these mechanical duplicators could produce copies in only relatively small batches, perhaps five hundred to a thousand copies at a time. Textual variants arose as each printer slightly altered the text.

An example of textual variants in a relatively modern text comes from the works of William Shakespeare written in Europe less than five hundred years ago. Shakespeare's plays were first printed in quartos, which were small books with the paper folded in half twice. They were later printed in folios, which were larger books with the pages folded in half once. The quarto and folio texts differ considerably from one another. The textual variants include different content, omission or inclusion of passages, and variant wording. Since none of Shakespeare's original manuscripts have survived, scholars must use the various manuscript witnesses to determine the text that is closest to the original text. Shakespearean scholars actually rely on biblical scholars in order to learn best practices in textual criticism.

The Shakespeare reader sitting on your bookshelf is composed of many manuscript witnesses and full of textual variants, even though William Shakespeare wrote only five hundred years ago.

Abraham Lincoln wrote the Gettysburg Address less than two hundred years ago. And even that has textual variants among the manuscripts. There are five different copies of the Gettysburg Address. (The excursus at the end of this chapter will go into greater detail.) Every one of these manuscripts is different from the others. There are textual variants between the address spoken by Lincoln, the printed copy in the newspaper, and the words etched on the Lincoln Memorial in Washington DC. These hallowed words are haplessly full of textual variants.

WHAT YOU NEED TO KNOW

The Bible is a collection of sixty-six different books written in different times and places by many different people. Like all ancient texts, the original manuscripts have not survived. Copies of the original manuscripts, known as manuscript witnesses, provide the biblical text. The thousands of manuscript witnesses provide compelling evidence that the Bible is trustworthy. Like nearly every text reproduced by hand or by mechanical duplication, there are textual variants in the biblical manuscripts. Textual variants are not always errors. Calling them errors is a misunderstanding of how texts have been reproduced throughout history. Textual criticism utilizes the manuscript witnesses in order to establish the best text. Compare the Bible to any other ancient text and it is the most historically attested, evidence-based, and trustworthy text in history.

CLAIM:

THE BIBLE CANNOT BE INERRANT, BECAUSE HUMANS WROTE IT.

Some of the claims made against the Bible are downright silly. This one is not. Whether you are skeptical of Scripture or a bold Bible believer, this claim deserves thoughtful reflection. Can something produced by human hands actually be free from error? Is it possible for mortal minds to speak the Word of God?

Experience would suggest that broken people create broken objects and think broken thoughts. Atomic bombs, guns, and grenades are human inventions. Human minds came up with the idea to cover blankets in smallpox so as to infect native tribes. Human hands crafted the iron shackles used to enslave people. And even the seemingly innocuous human creations—computers, phones, airplanes, or chemicals—reveal a hidden capacity for harm. Computers can be used to exploit vulnerable people. Phones can distract drivers. Airplanes can be turned into tools for terrorism. Chemicals can be carcinogens. Broken people can make only more brokenness, right?

It defies reason to think that God would use broken humans to compose a text that is trustworthy, inerrant, and authoritative. It seems impossible to think that human authors could be used to write the Word of God. A perfect and inerrant Bible that is God's Word of salvation cannot also be the product of sinful, broken people. There are two alternatives that seem far more reasonable:

Reject Human Authorship: Denying the influence of human authors is one way people have tried to resolve this issue. This notion suggests that the human authors of Scripture—Moses, David, Paul, John, and all the others—had no influence over the content of the biblical texts. According to this understanding, there is no remnant of Moses in Exodus and no personal influence of David in the Psalms. The arguments made in Romans are in no way Paul's arguments, and the peculiarities in the Gospel of John do not reflect any peculiarities in the person of John. The Word of God came through the human authors like water through a pipe. The Bible is inerrant because it is untainted by human hands.

Reject Divine Authorship: Others have attempted to resolve this issue by denying the divine authorship of the Bible. The claim is that human authors composed the Bible and therefore it is nothing more than a human book. It cannot be inerrant because Moses, David, Paul, and John were not inerrant people. Human authors err, human books err, and thus the Bible errs. This notion claims that the Bible was composed without the influence of God. It is a completely human book depicting the religious beliefs of a group of ancient people.

Every word of Scripture is inerrant as a result of the inspiration of the Holy Word.

Both of these alternatives attempt to resolve the mystery of a divinely inspired book written by human hands. And both of these alternatives are wrong. The Bible is both the inerrant Word of God and the work of errant human authors. Not one or the other. Both. This is possible only through the inspiration of the Holy Spirit. Without the inspiration of the Holy Spirit, the Bible would be nothing more than a human book. It could replace the phone book as a doorstop or booster seat for kids. However, every word of Scripture is inerrant as a result of the inspiration of the Holy Spirit. Inspiration and inerrancy are inextricable.

The work of the Holy Spirit in composing the Bible is more than merely inspiring authors and subject matter; the work of the Holy Spirit is to inspire every word of Scripture. The biblical authors repeatedly assert that the words of Scripture are the inspired Word of God:

- "All Scripture is breathed out by God and profitable for teaching, for reproof, for correction, and for training in righteousness, that the man of God may be complete, equipped for every good work" (2 Timothy 3:16–17).

- "For no prophecy was ever produced by the will of man, but men spoke from God as they were carried along by the Holy Spirit" (2 Peter 1:21).

- "And we also thank God constantly for this, that when you received the word of God, which you heard from us, you accepted it not as the word of men but as what it really is, the word of God, which is at work in you believers" (1 Thessalonians 2:13).

God used human authors to compose the inerrant Word of God. This does not, however, mean that God hijacked human bodies to write the Bible. It is abundantly clear that the biblical authors retained their own unique identities while being inspired by the Holy Spirit. Being carried along by the Holy Spirit allowed individual authors to maintain their individuality:

- Paul mentions his physical ailments: "So to keep me from becoming conceited because of the surpassing greatness of the revelations, a thorn was given me in the flesh, a messenger of Satan to harass me, to keep me from becoming conceited" (2 Corinthians 12:7).

- Luke suggests his personal preference for orderly accounts: "It seemed good to me also, having followed all things closely for some time past, to write an orderly account for you, most excellent Theophilus, that you may have certainty concerning the things you have been taught" (Luke 1:3–4).

- Peter includes personal greetings: "She who is at Babylon, who is likewise chosen, sends you greetings, and so does Mark, my son" (1 Peter 5:13).

God is the author of every word of Scripture. Every. Single. Word. Affirming that Scripture is God's Word, however, does not deny the presence of human authors. The inspiration of the Holy Spirit allowed human authors to proclaim the Word of God. Unlike anything else in all creation, the Bible is composed by human hands yet entirely divine and without error or contradiction. It is God's Word. And God's Word does not fail. It is powerful to create new life in the midst of death. It brings peace to storming souls, concerned consciences, and muddled minds. God's Word speaks eternal life into your past, present, and future. God makes a bold promise to work in and through the proclamation of the Word:

> For as the rain and the snow come down from heaven and do not return there but water the earth, making it bring forth and sprout, giving seed to the sower and bread to the eater, so shall my word be that goes out from my mouth; it shall not return to me empty, but it shall accomplish that which I purpose, and shall succeed in the thing for which I sent it. (Isaiah 55:10–11)

The Holy Spirit inspired every word of the Bible. This statement is true; however, this statement leaves many questions unanswered. Trust in the Bible is not built on sweeping statements without analysis. Rather, trust in the Bible is built on bold statements that can be dissected and discussed, explored and examined. This statement—"The Holy Spirit inspired every word of the Bible"—needs to be dissected.

HELLO! MY NAME IS HOLY SPIRIT

The Holy Spirit is the divine author of the Bible. Therefore, it is essential to have a firm knowledge of this person. The Holy Spirit is not a mere attribute or power of God. He is not a strange mist, vapor, or ghostly presence of a deceased person. He is the real and unique Third Person of the Trinity. He is the person Jesus promised to send: "Nevertheless, I tell you the truth: it is to your advantage that I go away, for if I do not go away, the Helper will not come to you. But if I go, I will send Him to you" (John 16:7).

The Holy Spirit is active and powerful. The Spirit was present in the beginning, "hovering over the face of the waters" (Genesis 1:2). The Spirit was active in the lives of Israel's judges and kings, enabling them to lead God's people with power and truth (Judges 6:34; 1 Samuel 16:13). Prophets spoke on behalf of God through the Spirit (Ezekiel 2:2–3; Micah 3:8). In the New Testament, the Holy Spirit was blasphemed against (Matthew 12:32), spoke on behalf of believers (Mark 13:11), and even betrayed (Acts 5:3). Jesus refers to the Holy Spirit as a Him. He confesses truth, comforts sorrow, and convicts sinners. The work of the Spirit proves that He is not a nebulous force but instead a real and unique person. And He is the divine author of the Bible.

The Bible is one continuous confession that Jesus is Lord.

The Holy Spirit directs and connects people to the death and resurrection of Jesus. He allows people to say and believe, "Jesus is Lord" (1 Corinthians 12:3). He unites sinners to Jesus through faith. Never pointing people to His own glory, the Holy Spirit is always pointing people to Jesus. This is crucial to understanding the inspiration of Scripture: the Holy Spirit points to Jesus. The Holy Spirit authored the Bible. Therefore, it makes sense that the Bible would also point to Jesus. Apart from the Holy Spirit, no one can truly confess that Jesus is Lord. Human authors could not have composed the Bible without the inspiration of the Holy Spirit. Why? Because the Bible is one continuous confession that Jesus is Lord.

The work of the Holy Spirit in composing the Bible was not limited to only inspiring the words of the biblical authors. He actively guided the composition of the Bible even before any writing occurred. The Holy Spirit guided the eyewitness interviews, organization, and preparation for writing. The canonization process was not devoid of the Spirit either; determining which books should be included in the Bible was done under the influence of the Holy Spirit. The Spirit is active and ongoing in all truth: "When the Spirit of truth comes, He will guide you into all the truth, for He will not speak on His own authority, but whatever He hears He will speak, and He will declare to you the things that are to come" (John 16:13).

EVERY WORD?

The Holy Spirit inspired the biblical authors before they wrote, while they were writing, and after they had written, ensuring that the right texts were included in the biblical canon. This raises some rather important and difficult questions: How can every word of the Bible be inspired if we do not have the original manuscripts? What about all the manuscript variants? How do we know which one is inspired by the Holy Spirit?

Before answering these questions, it is important to know a few things about ancient composition practices. People in the time of the New Testament, known as the Greco-Roman world, composed texts in a fairly similar way to modern writers. Authors would typically compose several copies of a text that were essentially rough drafts. Once a satisfactory rough draft had been composed, the writer would then read the text aloud and receive suggestions for changes. This means that a number of provisional texts were composed, and texts spent a long time in the composition process. It is highly unlikely that the Gospel of Luke was composed in one epic night of writing, and Paul likely composed multiple drafts of his Letter to the Romans. This means that there was a period of time when only half of the Gospel of Luke was written, and it also means that there were likely a number of versions of the Epistle to the Romans composed by Paul.

Each book of the Bible was composed over a period of time, with multiple rough drafts being utilized in the composition process. Does this negate the inspiration of the Holy Spirit? Not at all! The Holy Spirit worked in, with, and under the composition process of the biblical texts. Despite the multiple rough drafts and provisional texts, the biblical authors did eventually settle on a completed text. Eventually all the edits were completed, the revisions ceased, and the biblical authors settled on a final text. Luke eventually hit "Save" on the Gospel of Luke. Paul came to a point when he was ready to send his Epistle to the Romans. And the same is true for every other book of the Bible. Although there was a series of rough drafts, there was also one single final copy. This means that there was an original manuscript (autograph) from which other manuscript witnesses were copied. The Holy Spirit directly inspired the original text. Any copies of the original text share that inspiration insofar as they accurately reflect the original. Every word of the original manuscript is inspired; every word of every copy that does not deviate is also inspired.

The Bible consists of sixty-six books substantiated by at least twenty-five thousand ancient manuscript witnesses. Although none of the original manuscripts exist today, the sixty-six books of the Bible have been reconstructed by these ancient manuscript witnesses. Overwhelming evidence has shown that the copies of biblical manuscripts are accurate and do not deviate. And when there is a deviation in the manuscripts, scholars can recognize it and make sure that every word of the Bible remains accurate to the original text. Therefore, we can be confident that the Bible in its present form today is the inspired Word of God.

WHAT YOU NEED TO KNOW

It defies reason to think that God would use broken humans to compose a text that is trustworthy, inerrant, and authoritative. It seems impossible to think that human authors could be used to write the Word of God. Nevertheless, the Holy Spirit guided and inspired human authors to write the Bible. Every word of the original manuscript is inspired and inerrant; every word of every manuscript witness shares in that inspiration and inerrancy insofar as it accurately reflects the original manuscript. The Bible in its present form is composed of thousands and thousands of manuscript witnesses. These manuscript witnesses provide tremendous certainty that the copies accurately reflect the originals. All of this is to say: the Bible in your hand is the inerrant Word of God, inspired by the Holy Spirit, and written by human authors.

The Gettysburg Address

You cannot trust the Bible just because there are multiple manuscripts with variant readings. If you are going to honestly follow this logic, then you must in turn reject one of the greatest speeches in American history: the Gettysburg Address.

Abraham Lincoln delivered the Gettysburg Address on November 19, 1863, in response to the horrific carnage of the American Civil War. Lincoln spoke these words at the dedication of the Soldiers' National Cemetery in Gettysburg, Pennsylvania. The crowd gathered there that day immediately recognized that this address would have a profound effect on history. Lincoln's speech was later published by the Associated Press and etched in stone at the Lincoln Memorial in Washington DC.

There are, however, some massive problems with this massively influential speech. There are only five known copies of the Gettysburg Address. And all five have variant readings, making it unclear what Lincoln actually said at Gettysburg. Historians are divided over which version of the speech Lincoln presented on that momentous occasion. Some scholars believe that the true copy of the speech Lincoln used is lost forever. Although this moment in history occurred less than two hundred years ago, there are profound issues surrounding the various manuscripts of the Gettysburg Address:

Nicolay copy: This copy of the Gettysburg Address is named after John Nicolay, the president's top private secretary. Nicolay probably received this copy as a gift from the president. Historians agree that this is most likely the very first copy of the speech ever written. Lincoln wrote half of it in pen before leaving Washington and then finished the rest of the manuscript in pencil after arriving in Gettysburg. There were a number of reliable eyewitnesses close to Lincoln who recalled him arriving in Gettysburg and asking to be alone for the evening in order to finish the speech. Nevertheless, there is a great deal of uncertainty as to whether this manuscript was the one Lincoln held in his hand while giving the speech. There are a number of significant differences between the words of the Nicolay copy and the Associated Press's account of what Lincoln spoke publicly at the soldiers' cemetery.

Hay copy: This copy is named after John Hay, Lincoln's other private secretary, who likely received this copy as a gift from the president. Historians often consider this the second draft of the speech. However, there is little scholarly agreement as to exactly when this copy was written and whether this was the manuscript Lincoln used while giving the speech. Unlike the Nicolay copy, the Hay copy is written entirely in pen; it is also not folded in any way to suggest that Lincoln put it in his pocket (an important issue, because eyewitnesses to the speech saw

Lincoln take the manuscript out of his coat pocket). Nevertheless, dissenting scholars claim that this copy is closer to what Lincoln actually delivered and that he may have used the technique of a "soft crease" to fold the paper.

Everett copy: This third copy of the speech was clearly written after the address and is named after its recipient, Edward Everett. There is far less scholarly debate surrounding this copy. However, Lincoln did make a substantial change in it by adding the words "under God" and expanding the audience from America only ("that this government of the people") to an all-encompassing scope ("that government of the people"). These seemingly small changes had a substantial impact on the meaning and audience of the address.

Bancroft copy: Historians recognize this as the fourth draft of the Gettysburg Address. It is named after the American historian George Bancroft and includes a few minor word and punctuation changes from the Everett copy. This copy was supposed to be used for publication in a book; however, when the president wrote it, he left no room in the margins for a printer to reproduce the manuscript.

Bliss copy: One final copy of the Gettysburg Address, known as the Bliss copy, was penned for the purposes of mass publication on a lithograph machine. This manuscript is extraordinarily unique from the other copies penned by Lincoln. Unlike the other copies, Lincoln dated this one with the date of the address (November 19, 1863) and signed it with his first and last name. Scholars refer to this as the "autograph copy signed" version of the address. If there is a final copy of the speech, then this is it. This is also the copy of the address etched on the interior of the Lincoln Memorial in Washington DC.

This brief overview of the various manuscripts for the Gettysburg Address demonstrates something important: multiple manuscripts with variant read-

Multiple manuscripts with variant readings are common among historical texts.

ings are common among historical texts. The fact that there are minor variant readings among the many thousands of biblical manuscripts is not a reason to distrust Scripture. It is exactly the opposite. A lack of variant readings among the many different manuscripts would be cause for concern; since it is common for texts to change slightly as they are reproduced for different purposes, it seems appropriate that biblical manuscripts would show evidence of minor variant readings across the manuscripts.

And there is one more crucial element to notice: the Gettysburg Address is only one hundred and fifty years old, whereas the majority of biblical manuscripts are well over a thousand years older. A text that is quite young by historical standards—Lincoln's famous speech at Gettysburg—shows evidence of substantial changes. Text that is quite old by historical standards—the many books of the Bible—show evidence of only minor changes. Which text should be trusted more? Scripture clearly has the upper hand.

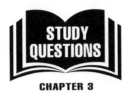

CHAPTER 3

1. Why might people intentionally try to find errors in the Bible?

2. Why is it important to learn about the manuscript witnesses that support the Bible?

3. There are significantly more New Testament manuscript witnesses than Old Testament manuscript witnesses. What caused this disproportionate number of manuscripts?

4. Is there any way that the existence of textual variants actually adds to the trustworthiness of the Bible?

5. The Bible was written fully by God but also fully by humans. What other aspects of the Christian faith share this same paradoxical tension?

6. The Holy Spirit connects people to Jesus. Why is it important to recognize the work of the Holy Spirit in writing the Bible?

7. What part of the composition process did the Holy Spirit inspire?

4

DISPUTES AND DISAGREEMENTS

History is like a family argument: everybody has an account of what happened, yet nobody can agree which account is right. Mom thinks that Jimmy knocked over the lamp with his football. Dad thinks the dog was wagging his tail and broke the lamp. Jimmy is convinced that the lamp spontaneously fell. And the dog just wants to be fed.

In all seriousness, this depiction of a family argument is a pretty accurate depiction of historical accounts. History is perspectival. The way one person depicts history is quite different from how another person depicts history. Columbus viewed his arrival to the new world differently than the indigenous people; European history and Mesoamerican history remember this event in radically divergent ways. Elisha Gray and Alexander Graham Bell certainly have different versions of how the telephone was invented. Postmodernity has recognized that history is deeply contextual and depends greatly on where the historian is situated in both time and space.

People have tried vehemently to discredit the history of the Bible. They have used every angle that you could imagine: The Bible concocts history as a sort of religious propaganda. The Bible is a chauvinistic, male-dominated rendition of history. Scripture is simply ancient Israelite nationalism. The Bible is concerned only with spiritual matters and therefore does not bother with accurately depicting historical events. This list could go on and on for days. . . .

The Bible accurately depicts historical events. It records God's work in human history; it is about the Creator interacting with His creation. Scripture is concerned with theology and history, spiritual and physical, God and humanity. Like all history, biblical history is told from a certain perspective. This does not, however, negate the fact that biblical history is trustworthy history.

CLAIM:

THE HISTORY IN THE BIBLE
CANNOT BE TRUSTED.

Answering this claim begins with one simple question: can other histories be trusted? Is any individual history—American, British, African, or Asian—an accurate and trustworthy depiction of reality? How you answer this question reveals your understanding of history.

Some people will claim that no history is accurate or trustworthy. Claiming that history cannot be trusted is a hallmark of relativism. This branch of philosophy claims that true and untrue, right and wrong, fact and fiction are strictly confined to the context that gives rise to them; what is true for one person is not true for another. Relativism makes a lot of sense in certain situations—one person can claim that peanut butter and jelly is the best sandwich and someone else can claim that it is the worst. (Don't even get me started on crunchy and smooth.) Both claims are right since this is a matter of personal taste and preference.

Relativism makes no sense in other situations: one person can claim that gravity draws objects downward toward the center of the earth while another can claim this is erroneous. If either person offers to resolve the matter by jumping out of the window, then the former claim will be affirmed and the latter claim will be proved dead wrong. Relativism is helpful in some situations and completely useless in others.

Relativism and history do not mix. Historical discourse attempts to describe events that took place in reality. History is about events occurring in time and space. It is not a matter of personal preference, individual inclination, or overt opinion. History recounts real happenings that occurred in real places, involving real people. It is simply wrong to argue that Archduke Franz Ferdinand was only scratched by a bullet and was not actually assassinated. It is flat wrong to claim that the Boston Tea Party was attempting to make a massive batch of cold brew rather than incite insurrection. When it comes to historical discourse, there is such a thing as true and untrue, right and wrong, fact and fiction.

This does not mean that all historical discourse is free from personal agendas, prejudices, and opinions. History is written from a certain perspective and point of view. This does not mean that all history is relative; it simply means that all history is written from the perspective of a person or group of people. Since all historical discourse is perspectival, it is important to carefully read and analyze these texts in order to understand how the author's perspective might have influenced the historical account.

ANALYZING BIBLICAL HISTORY

Analyzing a piece of historical writing relies on two important components—content and context. It is vitally important to investigate both the content and the context of historical discourse: Who wrote this historical tome? When was it written? Was there a specific purpose and audience for writing this historical record? What does it claim about a group of people?

Context can help reveal when a historical account is propaganda.

If a violent dictator commissions a historical account of his military prowess, we can certainly assume it will be a biased report. Texts written during a period of war will depict events differently than texts composed during a time of peace. Historical accounts written about a living person are markedly different from those looking back at the life of the deceased. The external factors—political, economic, military—giving rise to historical writing are vitally important for analyzing whether the account is trustworthy.

Content is another way to analyze historical discourse. Any history that exclusively praises one group of people while completely condemning another should be read with suspicion. A historical record that reveals no mistakes or shortfalls is likely biased. History written by the victors most likely excludes the voice of the defeated. For instance, it was a common practice in the ancient world to not give rival nations the respect of even mentioning them by name. Victorious nations would literally write their rivals out of history. These are most likely untrustworthy historical accounts.

Using both context and content to analyze the history in the Bible reveals that it is a trustworthy account. The historical context reveals that the Bible is not a history commissioned by a dictator, king, or ruler; instead, the history in the Bible was composed in the midst of slavery and freedom, subjugation and power, poverty and wealth. The historical content in the Bible is not exclusively praise or pompous acclaim; instead, the history in the Bible is full of military defeat, personal failure, and shady characters. Both the context and content of biblical history show that it is trustworthy.

CONTEXT

The history in the Bible is often dismissed because it was composed in the context of religion. Scholars have tried to argue that the history depicted in the Bible is inaccurate since religious texts are about theology and not history. This would be right if it were not so wrong. God works in and through His creation. Jesus is God entering into human time and space. This means that history and theology are inextricably connected. The Bible accurately reports historical events because it is about God working in human history. Inaccurate history would lead to inaccurate theology.

The first five books of the Bible—Genesis, Exodus, Leviticus, Numbers, and Deuteronomy—are traditionally attributed to Moses just before entering the Promised Land. The historical context of these books is not one of social power or military dominance; though the Israelites were no longer under the rule of the Egyptians, they were wandering in the wilderness without permanent land. This was certainly not history written by the victors; the Pentateuch was history written by former slaves on the run in the desert. Other parts of the Old Testament—the historical, poetic, and prophetic books— were written during times of strife, disunity, and exile. The people of Israel had more poverty than power, more struggle than success. The entire New Testament—Gospels and Epistles—were composed when the Church was underground and unsanctioned by the state.

The social and political context that gave rise to the Bible reveals that it was seldom written from a place of power. It is hard to silence the voice of another culture while having a sleepover with lions, like Daniel did. Destroying the history of other nations is difficult while being hauled off in captivity, as the exiles were. Holding to an entirely false history is foolishness when you are called to stand before the Roman Empire at the threat of death, like Paul was. The history in the Bible was not written from a palace or the center of power. The history in the Bible came from lions' dens and exile, prisons and underground house churches. This context shows that the history in the Bible should be trusted over the history composed by the Romans, Babylonians, or Egyptians. They wrote within the context of power; the biblical authors often wrote within the context of persecution.

Content

Analyzing the historical content in the Bible reveals that it is trustworthy. Histories that depict a person or nation as above error should be read with caution and suspicion. The heroes in the Bible are depicted with brutal honesty. Biblical history makes no effort to censor or improve public image:

- The Bible depicts Abraham, a central historical figure throughout the Bible, laughing at God's plans (Genesis 17) and lying that his wife is actually his sister (Genesis 20).

- The Bible portrays Sarah, a revered matriarch in Scripture, mistreating her servant Hagar (Genesis 16), laughing at God's plans for her life, and then lying about her actions (Genesis 18).

- The Bible remembers Moses, a powerful leader among the Israelites, as being an incompetent public speaker (Exodus 4), boldly defying God (Numbers 20), and being barred from entering the Promised Land (Deuteronomy 34).

- The Bible depicts David, the greatest king in the history of the Bible, as a murderer and adulterer (2 Samuel 11) who had a dysfunctional family (2 Samuel 17) and was a misguided leader (1 Chronicles 21).

- The Bible portrays Paul, author of many epistles in the New Testament, initially persecuting Christians (Acts 8) before becoming a follower of Jesus. Paul went out of his way to ensure that the historical record included his own shortcomings: "The saying is trustworthy and deserving of full acceptance, that Christ Jesus came into the world to save sinners, of whom I am the foremost" (1 Timothy 1:15).

Even the Book of Joshua, accused of being military propaganda and overt nationalism, proves to be trustworthy history. While recording the military success of Israel's campaign in the Promised

Land, the historical record includes personal failures and foreign heroes. Rahab, a Gentile prostitute from Jericho, is included not only in the history of Joshua (Joshua 2) but also in parts of the New Testament (Hebrews 11:31; James 2:25). Achan, an Israelite solider under Joshua's leadership, is recorded as inappropriately plundering a rival nation. His actions lead to widespread defeat in the Battle of Ai (Joshua 7). The history of the Bible lauds the work of the foreigner while being highly critical of its own people. Far from erasing counter-narratives, the history in the Bible gives voice to otherwise voiceless people. The historical content of the Bible is not censored, selective, or sterilized. It depicts military success and failure, leadership victories and blunders, community triumph and disappointment. There is no erasure of error in the historical content of the Bible. It is all there: good and bad, holy and evil, sin and salvation.

Analyzing the history in the Bible—both the context in which it arose and the content that it contains—provides evidence that it is trustworthy. It was neither written from a place of dictatorial power nor does it offer an unblemished account. These are powerful indicators of its historical reliability and accuracy.

ARCHAEOLOGICAL EVIDENCE

Archaeological excavations have also confirmed that the history in the Bible is trustworthy. Scholars have literally dug up the past and compared it to the history depicted in the Bible, thus upholding biblical events:

- The walls of Jericho (Joshua 6) have been unearthed to reveal a catastrophic destruction that aligns with the biblical depiction. There is both evidence of walls surrounding Jericho and evidence that those walls were rapidly destroyed in an event resembling an earthquake.

- An ancient inscribed stone, known as the Tel Dan Stele, provides extrabiblical evidence of King David and the House of

Israel. This memorial was prepared by a rival nation and confirms the kingship and military campaigns of King David. This discovery silenced any scholars attempting to deny the historical existence of David.

- A hardened clay seal from a signet ring, known as a bulla, was discovered with an inscription connecting it to the scribe Baruch, son of Neriah (Jeremiah 36:4). Ancient scribes would write a text and then seal it with a small lump of clay marked by a signet ring to prove that the document was unaltered. The discovery of this bulla confirmed the existence of this scribe mentioned in Scripture.

- Ancient burial containers, known as ossuaries, have been discovered and are believed to be linked to significant biblical figures such as Caiaphas and James the brother of Jesus.

Archaeologists continue to discover more ancient evidence confirming the veracity of the history in the Bible. Recent excavations at Jericho have confirmed the reliability of the biblical history depicting Joshua's conquests. This has not always been the case; previous archaeologists had rejected the Bible as unreliable and refused to use it as a tool for discovering ancient ruins. A British archaeologist, Kathleen Kenyon, led an excavation in the 1950s at Jericho and concluded that there were no walls surrounding the city at the time of Joshua's conquests. In fact, she and her team claimed that there was not even a city of Jericho during the time of Joshua and that any stories about conquering Jericho and destroying its walls were folklore and not fact.

More recent excavations have revealed many surprising discoveries. There is evidence of houses that were built into the walls of Jericho; this provides archaeological support for Rahab having a house incorporated into the fortification system (Joshua 2:15). Massive food remains in jars have also been found at Jericho; this suggests that destruction came to Jericho quickly rather than through a slower demise brought on by plague or pestilence. Lastly, excavations have revealed that Jericho had multiple walls that appear to have fallen at different times. Although a layer of fortification was likely destroyed during the Middle Bronze Age (1550 BC), another fortification surrounding the city was destroyed in the Late Bronze Age (1400 BC). The destruction of this wall aligns with the biblical history depicted in Joshua.

WHAT YOU NEED TO KNOW

The history in the Bible is trustworthy. Analyzing the social and political context in which biblical history was written reveals that it seldom came from a place of power; the history in the Bible often comes from lions' dens and exile, prisons and underground house churches. The content of biblical history also confirms that it is trustworthy. Histories that depict a person or nation as above error should be read with caution and suspicion; the heroes in the Bible are depicted with painful accuracy. There is no erasure of error in the historical content of the Bible. It is all there: good and bad, right and wrong, holy and evil. As if that is not enough, archaeologists have literally dug up the past and compared it to the history depicted in the Bible. The events depicted in the Bible are routinely upheld by archaeological discoveries. The history in the Bible can be trusted.

CLAIM:

THE GOSPELS DISAGREE ON EVEN THE MOST BASIC EVENTS IN THE LIFE OF JESUS.

There is an ancient proverbial story about four blind men and an elephant: The blind men encounter an elephant and attempt to determine what they are touching. Each man feels a different part of the elephant and reports a different account. The blind man who feels the elephant's leg determines that it is something like a pillar. The blind man who feels the tail reports feeling something similar to a rope. One of the men grabs the elephant's trunk and reports that it is a tree branch. The fourth blind man feels the elephant's belly and determines that there is some sort of wall in front of him. Although they are all touching the same animal, each man experiences and reports on a different part of the elephant.

This proverb is helpful in explaining the so-called "disagreements" regarding the life of Jesus in the Gospels. There are two versions of the Lord's Prayer that are markedly different from each other. The order of the temptations presented to Jesus in the wilderness varies between the Gospel of Matthew and the Gospel of Luke. The timeline of events surrounding Holy Week differs between the Gospels. Many people argue that these differing reports are proof that the Gospel writers simply got it wrong. Ironically, this line of argumentation simply gets it wrong.

Like the ancient proverb about the blind men and the elephant, four different authors composed the Gospels. They each encountered the life and ministry of Jesus in a way that was unique to their perspective. Just as the man feeling the elephant's leg had a different perspective than the man feeling the elephant's trunk, Matthew had a different perspective than John. The men feeling the elephant were all grappling with the same creature; however, their vantage point led them to describe it in markedly different ways. In the same way, different authors wrote the Gospels in order to address different audiences. It is woefully naïve to argue that their reports are incorrect simply because they pick up on different events and teachings of the life of Jesus. The Gospels are all the inspired and inerrant Word of God depicting the same Jesus Christ.

DIFFERENT AUTHORS; DIFFERENT AUDIENCES

Untangling the differences in the Gospels requires knowing something about the authors and audiences giving rise to these texts. Jesus engaged extremely diverse people to be His disciples. He gathered a socially and politically diverse group of followers. The disciples were not vanilla nor did they wear khaki or listen to soft rock. They were a colorful cross section of society: wealthy tax collectors, blue-collar fishermen, and religious zealots. These unique men had different cares and concerns. Their perspectives were not monochromatic. Their social networks were not the same; the followers of Jesus came from different communities and had ties to extremely different groups of people.

This radical diversity is seen in the Gospels. Different authors relied on different sources in order to write to different audiences for different purposes. To call these differences "inaccuracies" or "mistakes" is an inaccurate mistake. The genre and audience of the Gospels explains why the texts differ from one another:

Matthew: The Gospel of Matthew does not name an author in the text. Early Church writings, however, show that the disciple Matthew composed the text. Known also as Levi, Matthew was a Jewish tax collector with enough wealth and social connections to host a party in his house to honor Jesus (Mark 2:13–15). The Gospel of Matthew places an emphasis on Jewish religious practices and on Jesus fulfilling numerous Old Testament prophecies. The earliest copies of this text may have even been written in Hebrew rather than Greek. Matthew appears to have written his Gospel to the Jewish community in order to proclaim that the long-awaited Messiah had arrived in the person of Jesus.

Mark: The Gospel of Mark is also anonymous; there is no mention of an author in the text itself. Early Church writings connect the text to a colleague of Peter named Mark. The Gospel of Mark is the shortest of all the Gospels; whereas the Gospel of Matthew gives great detail about the temptation of Jesus, the Gospel of Mark mentions it in just a few sentences. The brevity and style of this text suggests that the author wrote it to be read aloud in one sitting. The audience for the Gospel of Mark was primarily Greek-speaking and unfamiliar with Jewish practices; the text often explains Jewish customs and translates Aramaic terms.

Luke: The Gospel of Luke, like the other Gospels, does not state an author in the text. Nevertheless, it does clearly state the author's audience and intention for writing. Luke the evangelist is identified in New Testament writings as a companion of Paul (Philemon 1:24), traveling missionary (2 Timothy 4:11), and medical physician (Colossians 4:14). He says that the text is written to a Greek Christian named Theophilus (Luke 1:3). Furthermore, Luke states that the genre in which he intends to write is an orderly narrative; readers are instructed to approach this text as an orderly narrative depicting the life and teachings of Jesus.

John: The Gospel of John is the last of the four Gospels in the New Testament. Early Church writings often quoted this text and attributed it to the disciple John. However, the Gospel of John is not considered to be one of the Synoptic Gospels. The word *synoptic* means similar or same view. The Synoptic Gospels—Matthew, Mark, and Luke—view the life and ministry of Jesus in the same way. The Gospel of John clearly has a different aim, placing a higher emphasis on the eternal truths of Jesus rather than linear history. The audience for the Gospel of John was less concerned with knowing exactly when events happened in the life of Jesus; rather, they were far more concerned with knowing why things happened in the life of Jesus.

This brief overview of the Gospels is far from exhaustive. Even this brief overview, however, provides enough insight to understand why different authors writing to different audiences would create markedly different texts. It is simply incorrect to treat these legitimate differences as if they were historical mistakes or miscalculations.

Claiming that the Gospels are flawed because they disagree on the most basic events in the life of Jesus is to prove that you do not understand the influences of genre or audience.

REFUTING THE SUPPOSED INACCURACIES

Skeptics have pored over the Gospels and attempted to find as many disagreements and discrepancies as possible. All they have really found, however, are situations in which different authors have arranged material in ways that are appropriate for their different audiences and purposes. Here are some responses to commonly cited "disagreements" in the Gospels:

Temptation of Jesus: A careful reading of how Matthew (4:1–11) and Luke (4:1–13) depict the temptation of Jesus will reveal a difference in the ordering of events. In Matthew, Satan tempts Jesus to turn stones into bread, then invites Him to leap from a high place, and lastly he offers Jesus all the kingdoms of the world. Luke orders the temptations differently: first Satan asks Jesus to turn stones into bread, then he encourages Jesus to claim the kingdoms of the world, and lastly there is the invitation to leap from the pinnacle of the temple in Jerusalem. This difference in the ordering of the last two temptations is often cited as proof that the Gospels do not accurately capture what happened in the life and ministry of Jesus.

There is, however, a rather obvious response to this claim that is found right in the text. Matthew connects the sequence of temptations with a conjunctive adverb (then), indicating an emphasis on sequence of events: "*Then* the devil took Him to the holy city and set Him on the pinnacle of the temple" (Matthew 4:5). Luke connects the various temptations of Jesus with a coordinating conjunction (and), indicating a list in no particular order: "*And* he took Him to Jerusalem and set Him on the pinnacle of the temple and said to Him, 'If You are the Son of God, throw Yourself down from here'" (Luke 4:9). Matthew places an emphasis on the chronological ordering of the events; Luke makes no indication that the list is supposed to be understood sequentially. Furthermore, Jerusalem is a reoccurring theme in the Gospel of Luke; it is no mistake that the final temptation of Jesus takes place in the holy city of Jerusalem.

The Lord's Prayer: Matthew and Luke present slightly different versions of the Lord's Prayer as well. Luke's version of the prayer is shorter than Matthew's: "Father, hallowed be Your name. Your kingdom come. Give us each day our daily bread, and forgive us our sins, for we ourselves forgive everyone who is indebted to us. And lead us not into temptation" (Luke 11:2–4). Matthew's version of the prayer includes an opening declaration that God dwells in heaven, requests that God's will be done on earth as it is in heaven, and concludes with an appeal for divine deliverance from evil (Matthew 6:9–13). Skeptics pounce on these differences and claim that this foundational prayer is built on shaky ground.

This false claim is undone with one simple question: do you think Jesus taught on prayer only once? No! Jesus taught extensively on the topic of prayer. He certainly spent a great amount of time instructing His disciples how to pray. It should also be noted that biblical prayers are not fixed incantations or formulaic statements. Ancient Jewish prayers (for example, an ancient Jewish prayer known as the Eighteen Benedictions) were abstracts or guides for how to pray. Jesus likely taught multiple versions of the Lord's Prayer to the disciples. Even if they were not identical, they were all guides given by Jesus for how to pray.

Holy Week: The final days of Jesus' life and ministry are the most highly scrutinized days of His entire life. Scholars have sifted and pored over the biblical texts in order to determine exactly how the events unfolded. And many have determined that the Gospels epically failed in their attempt to recount the events of Holy Week.

The argument is that the pieces do not fit when you try to put together the events of Holy Week as reported in Matthew, Mark,

Luke, and John. There is agreement about what happened up until about Wednesday of Holy Week. The Synoptic Gospels (Matthew, Mark, and Luke) report that the Last Supper occurred around this time, while Jesus was celebrating a Passover meal: "Then came the day of Unleavened Bread, on which the Passover lamb had to be sacrificed" (Luke 22:7). The Gospel of John, however, reports that the Last Supper occurred before the celebration of the Passover: "Now before the Feast of the Passover, when Jesus knew that His hour had come to depart out of this world to the Father, having loved His own who were in the world, He loved them to the end. . . . " (John 13:1). This makes it unclear not only on which day the Last Supper happened, but also when the subsequent trial and crucifixion of Jesus took place. Furthermore, many scholars are skeptical as to how both Jewish and Roman trials could take place between Thursday evening and Friday morning. These are commonly cited as inconsistencies and proof that the Gospels cannot be trusted.

This is quite troubling. That is to say, it is troubling until you know something about ancient calendars; then these supposed discrepancies disappear. There were no atomic clocks during the time of Jesus. Determining days and times was a local approximation rather than an exact science. Furthermore, there was not a universally accepted calendar to govern the days. There were multiple calendars in use during the time of Jesus: the Julian calendar, the Egyptian lunar and solar calendars, the Qumran solar calendar, and various other Jewish calendars. Just as different communities use different calendars today—Greek and Russian Orthodox churches use the Julian calendar whereas Catholic and Protestant churches use the Gregorian calendar—there were different calendars utilized by different communities during the time of Jesus.

It is reasonable to think that Matthew, Mark, and Luke were referencing one calendar while John was referencing an entirely different calendar. These texts were written for extremely diverse communities that likely gave preference to one calendar over another. There is evidence that various Jewish groups (Samaritans, Zealots, and the Essenes) utilized different calendars during the first century in Jerusalem. If the Gospels are referencing different calendars to suggest when the Last Supper occurred, then there is no real disagreement. They all agree on the same day for this momentous event; they simply utilize different reference points to mark when it occurred.

These are just a few of the most common arguments people use when claiming that the Gospels should not be trusted in their depiction of Jesus. There are many other arguments that people make. And there are many other perfectly reasonable explanations. It is a worthy endeavor to read the Gospels with a scrupulous mind and ask questions when the text is unclear. Nevertheless, trying to deconstruct the Gospels as historically inaccurate is a vain endeavor. It has been done before. And it has failed every time.

WHAT YOU NEED TO KNOW

Like the ancient proverb about the blind men and the elephant, four different authors with different perspectives composed the Gospels. They all grabbed on to a different part of the life and ministry of Jesus and reported the Good News from that perspective. This resulted in the radical diversity of accounts that appear in the Gospels. To accuse this diversity of being some sort of "inaccuracy" or "mistake" is an inaccurate mistake; different authors relied on different sources in order to write to different audiences for different purposes. Along these same lines, skeptics have pored over the Gospels and attempted to find as many disagreements and discrepancies as possible. All they have really found are situations in which different authors have arranged material in a way that is appropriate for their different audiences and purposes. Go figure!

William Shakespeare

William Shakespeare (1564–1616) is one of the most highly regarded authors in the western world. He wrote *Romeo and Juliet* (which means he pretty much wrote *West Side Story* as well), composed more than a hundred sonnets, and permanently influenced how people use language. As if that is not enough, Shakespeare even invented the word *bedazzled*. The man literally bedazzled the English language with his prose.

The brilliant bard wrote approximately thirty-eight plays. Ten of those plays are considered English history plays (eleven if you count *Edward III*, which was published anonymously). These plays depict real historical events that took place between 1397 and 1485. His plays recount historical events that occurred no more than two hundred years before his writing. Shakespeare was not depicting ancient history; he was depicting recent historical events that were separated from the present day by only a few generations. And these works are fraught with historical inaccuracies.

The historical depictions in Shakespeare's plays clash with the historical information available to scholars today. There are numerous places where the history presented by Shakespeare disagrees with the history presented in other reputable sources. This has led historians to debate whether Shakespeare was inaccurate in his knowledge or intentionally emphasizing one point over another. Was he a really good playwright but a really bad historian? Or was he representing history in such a way as to convey a specific meaning to his audience?

There are numerous instances in which Shakespeare nuances history for literary purposes. Historians agree that Henry VI was not nearly as saintly as Shakespeare presents him. Humphrey, Duke of Gloucester, was apparently far more haughty and ambitious in real life than he appears on stage. There are other discrepancies as well: *Henry IV* depicts a relationship between Prince Hal and his father that is rife with conflict. This is an exaggeration of the real relationship between the two men. Historians also agree that the rivalry between Hal and Hotspur did not actually resemble the depiction presented by Shakespeare. This is an incomplete list that could be filled with many more examples of Shakespeare's historical inaccuracies.

There are, however, instances in which Shakespeare accurately depicted real historical events. For example, Shakespeare portrayed Richard II as giving a mournful soliloquy in which he says, "For God's sake let us sit upon the ground/And tell sad stories of the death of kings" (*Richard II* 3.2.155–56). This speech is quite similar to an eyewitness account reported by Adam of Usk. It appears that the real Richard II gave this speech after dinner during his imprisonment in the Tower of London. Shakespeare curiously relocates

this historical speech by putting it in an entirely new location in time and space.

These historical inaccuracies are not merely mistakes. Shakespeare was not seeking to convey only history in his writing. He fused drama and history, poetry and politics. There is no denying that the historical plays of Shakespeare are based on real, historical events. There is also no denying that he arranged the historical events, emphasized certain points, and skimmed over other historical events in order to convey a specific meaning. Does this mean that Shakespeare was bad at history? No. Does this mean that Shakespeare was unaware of these discrepancies? No. Does this mean that Shakespeare was recounting historical events in a certain way in order to make a specific point? Yes.

What does this have to do with the Bible? Like Shakespeare, the Gospels have been accused of historical inaccuracies. Just as Shakespearean history emphasizes certain realities and glosses over others, the Gospels highlight certain aspects of history and barely mention others. Furthermore, there are seeming disagreements in the historical record: There are two versions of the Lord's Prayer that are markedly different from each other. The order of the temptations presented to Jesus in the wilderness varies between the Gospel of Matthew and the Gospel of Luke. The timeline of events surrounding Holy Week differs between all the Gospels. The very same accusation that is thrown on Shakespeare is thrown on the authors of the Gospels: they must have been really bad historians in order to get all of these facts wrong.

Nevertheless, it is obvious that the Gospels are not a historical account of the Roman Empire or the Jewish people. They are a historical account of the Son of God, Jesus Christ. They are not history for the sake of history; they are history for the sake of the Good News of Jesus Christ. Their aim is not to report every single detail of what happened; their aim is to proclaim the Gospel so that broken sinners can receive the forgiveness of sins. This is a substantial difference.

There appear to be disputes and disagreements regarding the basic events in the life of Jesus. The authors of the Gospels were inspired by the Holy Spirit to reveal the theological meaning behind historical events.

These texts are more than just human history. The Gospels are about God's work in human history. Differences in the ordering of events, details that appear in one Gospel but not another, and wordings that do not exactly match up are not simply errors. This is not evidence that the Gospels are the result of shoddy work by helpless historians. This is evidence that God used different authors to make different theological points. The Gospels do not report history apart from God's work of salvation. Rather, the Gospels set history in the context of salvation.

The Gospels set history in the context of salvation.

It is foolhardy to accuse Shakespeare of being a bad historian. His point was not to write history simply for the sake of history; he was writing historical plays that conveyed literary meaning. It is equally foolhardy to accuse the Gospels of containing bad history. They proclaim the good news that God has come into human history in the person of Jesus Christ so that the dead may live.

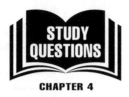

CHAPTER 4

1. What are some arguments people have made in order to discredit the history contained in the Bible?

2. How does the Bible prove these arguments incorrect?

3. Are there other ways the history in the Bible is proved accurate?

4. How did differences in audience influence the contents of the Gospels?

5. Why is it important to know how to refute the supposed inaccuracies in the Gospels?

6. Should Christians ask difficult questions about the historical timeline of the Gospels?

7. How are the historical accounts in Shakespeare's plays similar to historical accounts in the Gospels?

5

DECEIT AND DECEPTION

Parlor tricks are fun. Talented tricksters can ask someone to pick a card, shuffle that card back into the deck repeatedly, and then make the card amazingly reappear. And that is not all. Coin tricks can make a coin seemingly disappear and turn up behind your ear. In another parlor trick, a spectator shuffles a deck of cards and somehow ends up with every card face down except for the aces. These tricks all rely on sleight of hand: a trickster subtly diverts attention away from one thing and toward something else. When nobody is looking, a card or coin is taken out or added, placed under the table or up a sleeve in order to make the trick work. Parlor tricks are fun as long as they stay in the parlor.

However, you do not want your doctor to do sleight of hand. Hiding a medical report up her sleeve will not make your diabetes go away; shuffling the deck repeatedly and hoping the test results disappear is bad medicine. You do not want your banker to do sleight of hand. Counting out bills and making a twenty vanish before your eyes is no fun; turning your student loan interest rate from a three to a six is a pretty lame trick. There are countless other places—auto repair shop, dentist, grocery store, subway—where you do not want sleight of hand to happen. Parlor tricks are fun as long as they stay in the parlor.

The Bible is accused of being one big parlor trick. Cynics claim that there were many other books that should have been included in the Bible, but the Church made them simply disappear. These skeptics argue that the Church used sleight of hand to hide these other texts. Going behind a curtain, they shuffled the deck and somehow made certain texts vanish from the biblical canon. This accusation misrepresents how the biblical canon came into existence. There is ample evidence to refute this claim and others like it.

CLAIM:

A SMALL GROUP IN THE EARLY CHURCH PICKED THE BOOKS OF THE BIBLE BEHIND CLOSED DOORS.

Juicy scandals can draw a crowd. Gossip, intrigue, and rumors get people talking. Secrets, schemes, and deception make for a really good story. Open and honest deliberation, on the other hand, causes people to yawn. Transparency and truth are all too often overlooked as being boring. Books and documentaries, scholars and researchers have tried hard to turn the Bible into a scandalous scheme concocted by the Church. They claim that the biblical canon came together secretly and illegitimately. This story line, though erroneous and untrue, certainly draws a crowd.

The claim typically goes something like this: There were many different religious texts that deserved to be in the Bible. These texts included the Acts of Peter, Acts of John, the Gospel of Thomas, the Gospel of Peter, and the Gospel of Mary. There was even a Gospel of Judas (gasp!). Before Christianity became the official state religion of Rome, various Christian congregations freely and openly used many of these texts. Nobody spoke out against their usage until roughly AD 325, after Constantine became the first Christian emperor of the Roman Empire. For political reasons, he demanded that there be one official biblical canon since Christianity was to become the official state religion. Constantine authorized an exceedingly small group of church leaders to meet secretly and determine which books were to be included in the canon and which books were to be burned. They emerged from this meeting with the Bible and a list of banned books. Therefore, the Bible you have in your hand today is the result of a scandalous cover-up by the Church. Anybody adhering to these banned books was forcibly silenced and suppressed. Anybody speaking out against this process was killed or tortured.

Pretty juicy, huh?

The way the Bible was really formed is far less scandalous. (Perhaps that makes it far less interesting for scholars trying to sell books.) Here is a rather broad overview of how the biblical canon came into existence: Following the resurrection and ascension of Jesus, the disciples went in various directions and proclaimed the Gospel of Jesus Christ. Preaching and teaching, baptizing and catechizing, the disciples established Christian worshiping communities. These Christian communities were considered a sect within Judaism, meeting in the temple and synagogues and using the Old Testament texts as their Scripture for preaching and teaching. These communities of Jesus-followers began to exchange letters written by the apostles among the various communities. These letters, also known as epistles, provided teaching and encouragement for the followers of Jesus. Narratives about the life and ministry of Jesus were also written and began circulating throughout Christian communities.

These Christian texts circulated across vast geographic spaces. During the first century, the apostle Paul's letters began to circulate as a collection. During the second century, the four Gospels began to circulate as a collection. These texts then began to circulate collectively rather than individually. There is evidence that the major portions of the New Testament were established as early as the second century. Although there were other texts present during this time, the Christian communities recognized them as inaccurate. The Church freely and openly discussed whether these texts ought to be used in worship and catechesis.

There are many examples from the Early Church indicating how these nonbiblical texts were handled. At the end of the second century, a bishop in Asia Minor had to lead one of his congregations in determining which texts to use in worship. The bishop was Serapion of Antioch and the text was the Gospel of Peter. When Serapion was first placed in his bishopric around AD 190, he discovered that one of his congregations routinely read the Gospel of Peter in worship. Having never read the text for himself, Serapion had to simply trust the orthodoxy of his parishioners. He decided to take a pastoral approach and tell his congregation that if this was the only thing threatening division among them, it could be read in worship.

Then Serapion finally got around to reading the so-called gospel. He found that the Gospel of Peter was abounding in falsehood; it included such things as a talking cross that floated around while making a post-resurrection appearance at Jesus' tomb and freakishly tall angels with heads that reached into the heavens. Adding to Serapion's suspicions was the author—or lack thereof—behind the Gospel of Peter. Despite the gospel's name, Peter did not write the text. Rather, someone claiming to be Peter wrote the text.

Serapion recognized that this text was *pseudepigraphic.* This means that the so-called gospel falsely attributed Peter as the author. He warned his congregation that it was falsely inscribed with Peter's name and told them not to use it anymore. In the end, however, it was not the absurdly tall angels or the falsely ascribed authorship that Serapion cited when he rejected the use of the Gospel of Peter in worship. Serapion rejected the text's use in worship for a far more basic reason: the text had not been handed down for that purpose. Serapion stated that the text should be rejected simply on the basis that it was not handed down by previous generations of believers as a biblical text. Not one of his predecessors had acknowledged the Gospel of Peter as fit for use in worship. Therefore, Serapion was not going to authorize the text's use either. The text was not fit for use in worship because Christendom had never used it that way.

CARDS ON THE TABLE

This example makes it clear that there was no scandal or secrecy involved in determining which texts should be included in the Bible. Instead, the formation of the biblical canon was openly discussed and entirely transparent. Rather than secret decisions about which books were included or excluded, the Early Church put all the cards on the table for everyone to see. The Church fully explained how each book of the Bible came to be included in the biblical canon. The Church utilized different categories when classifying various texts:

Homologoumena: These were texts unanimously included in the biblical canon. There were no disputes or disagreements as to whether these texts deserved to be in the Bible based on author, content, and widespread usage among congregations. Some examples of these books include the four Gospels, the Acts of the Apostles, and the Epistles of Paul.

Antilegomena: These were texts that some disagreed about in regards to their canonical status. There were some church leaders or congregations that did not consider these texts a part of the biblical canon because there were questions about author, content, or usage among congregations. Some examples of these books are the Epistle of James, Jude, and 2 Peter.

Heretical: There was unanimous agreement that these texts were not fit to be included in the biblical canon because they were incorrect, inaccurate, or part of an entirely separate religious community. Some examples of these texts include the Gospel of Peter, the Gospel of Thomas, and the Acts of Andrew.

Determining the biblical canon was not a closed conspiracy. Rather, it was a deliberate dialogue that took place over many generations. There are a few crucial highlights in the canonization process that are worth knowing:

Early Church Writings. The Early Church was geographically diverse with various communities dispersed across hundreds of miles. As a result of this dispersion, church leaders used letters and other writings to communicate across the various Christian communities. These texts provide evidence of the active and open conversations that took place regarding which books were included in the biblical canon. Eusebius of Caesarea wrote a detailed history of the Early Church entitled *Ecclesiastical History* that was completed around AD 325. This text gave a detailed overview of which texts were undisputed, disputed, and rejected by the Early Church. Around the same period of time, another church leader named Athanasius included a listing of the twenty-seven books of the New Testament in his Festal Letter (AD 367). Various Early Church meetings in Africa—Hippo Regius (AD 393) and Carthage (AD 397)—further confirmed the twenty-seven books of the New Testament.

The Council of Nicaea. This council, convening in Nicaea in AD 325, was a major milestone for the Early Church for many different reasons, but it had nothing to do with the canonization of the Bible. It has been alleged that this was when the Church determined which books were to be included in the Bible and which books were to be burned. In actuality, this council convened at the request of the Roman Emperor Constantine I in order to discuss debates about the divinity of Jesus that were introduced by a theological movement known as Arianism. This council resulted in the creation of the Nicene Creed. No record or evidence exists indicating that an extensive discussion took place on which books should be included in the Bible and which books should be excluded. Yet there was even a myth formulated long after the council stating that various books were placed on an altar and the books that spontaneously fell off were banned. Do not let anyone fool you—this is not how the books of the Bible were determined. This rendition of the canonization process is as legitimate as Paul Bunyan and Babe the Blue Ox.

Codex Sinaiticus. Discovered at St. Catherine's Monastery near Mount Sinai, this is an exceptionally early collection of biblical texts dating back to about AD 330–60. This text contains many books of the Old Testament and New Testament together. Although it is fragmented as a result of age, the text does provide firm evidence that the majority of the biblical canon was set by the fourth century. Codex Sinaiticus also provides extremely early evidence of how the various books of the Bible were arranged by the Early Church. This refutes any claims that the biblical canon was determined well into the Middle Ages.

Jerome's Vulgate. This is a Latin translation of the Bible composed in AD 382 at the request of Pope Damasus I. Although many others contributed to this endeavor, Jerome was the primary translator for this text. Drawing from Hebrew Old Testament texts and Greek New Testament texts in order to create an updated Latin translation, the Vulgate became the authoritative translation in the West. This persisted through the Middle Ages and into the sixteenth century. One striking feature of the Vulgate is that it labeled a group of texts "apocryphal" since they were included only in the Septuagint (a Greek translation of the Old Testament) and were excluded from the Hebrew text. By doing this, Jerome separated these texts from the rest of the biblical canon and determined them to be of secondary status.

The Reformation. This might seem a bit out of place in a listing of highlights about the formation of the biblical canon. All the other highlights are quite early in the history of the Church; the Reformation did not take place until the sixteenth century. However, the biblical canon continued to develop even into this period of history. Some major occurrences happened as a result of the Reformation and these profoundly shaped the biblical canon. One such change was the invention of the printing press, enabling mass production of Bibles. This new technology allowed for considerably larger print runs of the Bible, which had a profound impact on the biblical canon by standardizing which books were included in the Bible and in what order they appeared. Before the moveable-type printing press, Bibles were produced in rather small batches and were inaccessible to many people. In fact, Bibles were so rare and valuable in the Middle Ages that they were literally chained to the table in a library to avoid theft. With the invention of the printing press, however, Bibles became more accessible at a much lower price. The advent of the printing press was deeply influential on the formation of the biblical canon.

There are many other highlights that could be mentioned in the history of how the Bible was formed. These are just a few of the noteworthy occurrences. What is apparent from these highlights is that the formation of the biblical canon was not top-down, authoritarian, or isolated to a single moment in history. There were no backroom negotiations as to what books were in and what books were out. There is no single moment at which point the canonical books of the Bible were once and for all determined. The majority of the biblical canon was set by the fourth century, before the Church was granted any sort of political or social standing in ancient society; the outer limits of the biblical canon continued to be debated long after Christianity was granted status as the official state religion. In a strange paradox, the formation of the Bible occurred rapidly and really slowly. Nevertheless, the work of the Holy Spirit has permeated the entire process—guiding the composition of the Word of God, overseeing the inclusion of texts into the biblical canon, and breathing divine power into translations.

WHAT YOU NEED TO KNOW

The Bible was not made behind a curtain. The question of which books to include was not answered by putting them on an altar and waiting for some to fall down. There were no card tricks or sleight of hand that went into the formation of the biblical canon. Rather, guided by the Holy Spirit, the Church went about the communal process of determining which books were to be included in the Bible. This process began with local congregations utilizing texts in worship and circulating letters written by the apostles. The Gospels and the majority of the Epistles of Paul, Peter, and John were considered authoritative and canonical quite early in the history of the Church (circa fourth century). These were the *homologoumena* texts about which nobody expressed uncertainty regarding their place in the Bible. Other texts, known as *antilegomena*, were openly debated and discussed amid the Early Church as to whether they merited inclusion in the Bible. The vast majority of the biblical canon—both Old Testament and New Testament—was settled by the fourth century. The outer limits of the canon—the Apocrypha, Hebrews, James, Jude, and Revelation—were debated into the Reformation.

Do not let anyone fabricate stories about the Church going behind a curtain, shuffling the deck, and somehow making certain texts appear in the biblical canon. This accusation misrepresents how the biblical canon came into existence. This claim simply gets it wrong. There are thousands of letters, councils, and commentaries from the Early Church to prove that the biblical canon was formed through open and honest communal deliberation guided by the Holy Spirit.

CLAIM:

THE EARLY CHURCH SECRETLY WORKED TO SILENCE CERTAIN NONBIBLICAL TEXTS.

Some scholars have claimed that the Church worked especially hard to censor other texts and silence certain voices. This argument suggests that the early followers of Jesus agreed on a certain story about the ministry of Jesus and refused to let anyone speak a dissenting opinion. In order to destroy these unorthodox views, the Early Church burned the texts and banned them from seeing the light of day.

There is one big, glaring problem with this argumentation: all of the texts referred to by the people making these arguments still exist today. You can walk into any bookstore or library and find the Gnostic gospels. You can search for them on the Internet and find literally thousands of ancient texts presenting a nonbiblical view of Jesus. If the Church attempted to censor these texts, then they did a really bad job of it. Had the Church truly set out to burn all the writings of dissenting voices, they must have inadvertently missed a few thousand of them. If the followers of Jesus really went out of their way to silence these unorthodox voices, it would seem a bit odd that these voices are still speaking today.

There are many ancient nonbiblical texts in existence today that offer a depiction of Jesus. Although these writings describe the life and teachings of Jesus, they were not included in the Bible. There are literally hundreds of texts like this in antiquity. Here are a few of the most important kinds of these writings:

Apostolic Writings. There are many Early Church writings that were not included in the Bible. For instance, strong evidence suggests that Paul wrote more than two letters to the Corinthians. He writes in 1 Corinthians, "I wrote to you in my letter not to associate with sexually immoral people" (5:9).

He references a previous letter to the Corinthians that is not included in the Bible. Paul also mentions something note-worthy in 2 Corinthians: "Even if I made you grieve with my letter, I do not regret it" (7:8). This seems out of place since 1 Corinthians does not have a particularly harsh tone that would cause such sorrow. Therefore, many scholars believe that 1 Corinthians is at least Paul's second letter to the Corinthians and 2 Corinthians is more likely Paul's fourth letter to the Corinthians. There is no reason to believe that the Church purposefully excluded these texts from the Bible; rather, the Church simply did not use and circulate these other letters in the same way they used 1 and 2 Corinthians. It is likely that Paul is not the only apostle who wrote letters not included in the Bible. Peter and John probably also wrote other letters that were not included in the biblical canon. The description of the life and teachings of Jesus in these "lost" letters was un-doubtedly parallel to that which is presented in the Gospels and other New Testament writings.

Early Church Writings. The Early Church produced many other nonbiblical texts and statements depicting the life and teach-ings of Jesus. One important text is the *Didache*, a catechism from the mid-to-late first century. This text describes worship practices in the Early Church, depicts communion practices quite similar to what is described in Corinth, and provides instructions for Christians and a handful of common prayers (including the Lord's Prayer). Another important Early Church text is *The First Apology* written by Justin Martyr. One of the earliest defenders of the faith, Martyr wrote in the early to middle second century. His writings discuss many of the teachings of Jesus; he describes at length statements made by Jesus concerning civil government, chastity, Baptism, and the resurrection. Martyr states that these are drawn from the "memoirs of the apostles," a reference to the Gospels. Finally, the Apostles' Creed is an important Early Church statement about the life and work of Jesus. The Apostles' Creed was derived from other earlier creeds dating back to the earliest days of the Church. All these texts—the *Didache*, the writings of Justin Martyr, and the Apostles' Creed—were excluded from the biblical canon. The Early Church recognized them as being helpful texts depicting the life and teachings of Jesus yet still did not include them in the New Testament.

Gnostic Writings. Like the texts described above, many Gnostic texts were not included in the biblical canon. Yet unlike the previously mentioned texts, these texts were excluded from the Bible because they grossly distorted the life and teachings of Jesus. Gnosticism describes an ancient religion that rejected the material world as inferior and downright evil and sought the discovery of secret knowledge. The name *Gnostic* derives from the Greek word for "knowledge"; this religious sect was fixated on hidden wisdom and secret knowledge that led to salvation. The Gnostics latched on to small portions of the life and teachings of Jesus while also inserting many other teachings of their own. For instance, the Gospel of Thomas includes many distortions of Jesus' teachings. Whereas the canonical Gospels record Jesus teaching His followers that they will be persecuted (Matthew 5:10–11; Luke 6:22; John 15:18–25), the Gospel of Thomas includes this teaching while also inserting a teaching about bringing forth what is from within in order to be saved (No. 70). As previously mentioned in this chapter, the Gospel of Peter depicts the resurrection of Jesus in a highly distorted manner, complete with a talking cross and angels with heads reaching into the sky. This is especially characteristic of Gnostic texts: they conflate and confuse the true teachings of Jesus by inserting false Gnostic teachings.

Therefore, these texts were excluded from the biblical canon with good reason: they were neither Christian nor accurate.

Gnostic writings came out of an entirely different religious faction with an entirely different conception of divinity, creation, and evil. There is no reason the Early Church would include Gnostic texts in the Bible. This would be like a handbook on welding including an entire section on the art of basket weaving. It is simply out of place. Besides the fact that Gnostic writings came out of an entirely different religion, there is also an obvious inattention to historicity. Many Gnostic writings present an isolated depiction of Jesus that cannot be confirmed by any other sources—even other Gnostic texts! What happens in one Gnostic gospel does not happen in another; the Gospel of Philip and the Gospel of Peter seem to depict a totally different Jesus in word and deed.

These examples—ranging from Paul's many letters to the Church in Corinth to the completely absurd Gnostic writings—show that there were many different texts depicting the life and teachings of Jesus that were not included in the Bible. These "excluded" texts were largely the work of Christian writers, as in the case of Justin Martyr and the *Didache*; however, some of these excluded texts were the work of entirely different religious sects as in the case of the Gnostic writings. The point is that there is nothing scandalous about the existence of nonbiblical texts. The Early Church was not trying to hide anything: Jesus clearly did not have a secret mistress, nor did He extol secret teachings to a fortunate few. There was no conspiracy or confidential texts. What really happened to the texts that were excluded from the Bible is far from shocking, scandalous, or surprising.

The Early Church was not trying to hide anything.

WHAT REALLY HAPPENED?

Nothing. (I told you it was not scandalous!) The Early Church openly and plainly determined that some texts should not be included in the biblical canon. And they made their determinations known to all people. When the Early Church flatly rejected a text as coming from a different religion, they clearly stated their basis for doing so. When the Early Church accepted a text as useful but not biblical, they made sure people knew that was how the text was to be received. When there was some uncertainty about whether a text should be included in the Bible, the various Christian communities had open and robust debates about the matter.

How do we know this is what really happened? We have ample historical evidence. The writings of the Early Church reveal that there was no deceit or deception when it came to determining the truth about the life and teachings of Jesus. For instance, the Early Church made it clear when they disagreed with a certain teaching: "They who maintain the wrong opinion say that there is no resurrection of the flesh."[3] Neither was it a secret that there were Gnostic texts attempting to shoulder their way into the Church. Origen, an influential Early Church writer, left no room for deceit or deception when he called for someone to refute these false teachings:

> I see the heterodox assailing the holy Church of God in these days, under the pretence of higher wisdom, and bringing forward works in many volumes in which they offer expositions of the evangelical and apostolic writings. . . . It appears to me, therefore, to be necessary that one who is able to represent in a genuine manner the doctrine of the Church, and to refute those dealers in knowledge, falsely so-called, should take his stand against historical fictions, and oppose to them the true and lofty evangelical message.[4]

---

3   Justin Martyr, *On the Resurrection* 2 (*Anti-Nicene Fathers* 1:294).
4   Origen, *Commentary on the Gospel of John* 5 (*Anti-Nicene Fathers* 9:348).

There was clearly no sort of backroom burning of banned books in the Early Church. Rather, they openly and honestly disagreed when someone taught falsely about the life and teachings of Jesus. No parlor tricks. No secretly making books disappear. Instead, there was candid dialogue about which books ought to be included in the Bible and which books ought to be left out.

The Early Church formed the New Testament canon with a great deal of transparency. As mentioned previously in this chapter, Eusebius wrote a detailed text entitled *Ecclesiastical History* in which he explained which books were accepted as biblical, which books were disputed, and which books were flatly rejected. After mentioning the books unanimously accepted into the New Testament canon, he explained which books of the Bible garnered some further discussion:

> Among the disputed writings, which are nevertheless recognized by many, are extant the so-called epistle of James and that of Jude, also the second epistle of Peter, and those that are called the second and third of John, whether they belong to the evangelist or to another person of the same name.[5]

Cards face up and on the table, Eusebius lays it all out there for people to know what happened. And then he goes on to explain why certain books were rejected from the biblical canon:

> And further, the character of the style is at variance with apostolic usage, and both the thoughts and the purpose of the things that are related in them are so completely out of accord with true orthodoxy that they clearly show themselves to be the fictions of heretics. Wherefore they are not to be placed even among the rejected writings, but are all of them to be cast aside as absurd and impious.[6]

---

5   Eusebius, *Ecclesiastical History* 3 (*Nicene and Post-Nicene Fathers Series* 2, 1:156).
6   Eusebius, *Ecclesiastical History* 3 (*Nicene and Post-Nicene Fathers* Series 2, 1:157).

Deceit and deception within the Early Church is a lie. The process of establishing which books ought to be included in the Bible was the farthest thing from crooked conspiring and deceitful deceiving. Rather, it was transparent and honest communal deliberation guided entirely by the Holy Spirit.

Deceit and deception within the Early Church is a lie.

WHAT YOU NEED TO KNOW

It is impossible to argue that the Early Church worked to secretly silence nonbiblical texts, because these texts presently exist. The presence of Early Church writings explaining how and why they rejected these texts is further proof that there was not a secret movement to silence them. Instead, the Church openly and honestly disagreed with these texts because they came out of a different religious movement and espoused an entirely different view of the life and teachings of Jesus.

There is nothing scandalous about the "excluded" texts that were left out of the Bible. There were letters written by the apostle Paul that were excluded from the Bible. The Apostles' Creed and other orthodox Early Church writings were excluded from the Bible. The Holy Spirit guided the Church to exclude these texts not because their content was incorrect but simply because they were not meant to be part of the Bible. There were other texts—largely written by a separate religious movement known as Gnosticism—that were also excluded because their content was grossly inaccurate and inconsistent with the life and teachings of Jesus. The Church clearly did not destroy these books, because they remain in existence today.

If you are looking for a scandal, then you will have to look elsewhere. The Early Church did not hide behind a curtain to create the Bible. Nobody hid any secret books up their sleeve. All the cards were set down on the table for everyone to see.

EXCURSUS

Gnostic Gospels

Proteus was a wily character in Greek mythology. It is hard to know exactly what Proteus was since he could change forms in an instant: he could shift from the form of a serpent to a lion to a bear—and then back to a serpent. The moment you thought you had Proteus figured out was the very moment he would change forms again.

The ancient religion of Gnosticism is a lot like Proteus. Rather than possessing one single form, the Gnostics came in a variety of different forms that comprised a colorful panoply of beliefs. Scholars once thought they had fully comprehended this ancient religion. However, like Proteus, a trove of new evidence—the Nag Hammadi library—has changed how this religion is understood. It appears that modern historians are less certain about Gnosticism than ever before.

A discovery in the Egyptian town of Nag Hammadi in 1945 had a profound influence on modern understandings of this religion. Two brothers uncovered a large library of ancient texts while digging for fertilizer. The discovery contained more than fifty different texts that were from a Gnostic community. Although some of these texts were destroyed when their mother burned them (thanks, Mom!), the majority of them are now in the possession of scholars and historians. This discovery answered some questions about Gnosticism while raising many more.

There are, nevertheless, a few key facets of Gnosticism that are certain. The various Gnostic communities in the ancient world were adamant about rejecting the material world as inferior, inadequate, and imperfect. The physical world was believed to be the defective work of a defective demiurge. Matter, flesh, and bodies were considered innately bad. The spiritual realm, however, was free from corruption and therefore far superior. Gnosticism was founded on the basic premise that one must ultimately escape the material realm in order to obtain enlightenment. This was a central tenant of the religion.

Another common element of ancient Gnostic communities is their emphasis on secret knowledge as the path to salvation. Hidden wisdom was the key to transcending the material world. Secret wisdom could release the remnant of god within you—known as the inner spark of the divine—and set you free from the material world. This redemptive knowledge was not accessible to all people; only certain individuals could possess this wisdom. If you acquire the right secrets, then you could enjoy enlightenment. Otherwise you were simply stuck in a prison of flesh.

Why should you care at all about this ancient religion? Is this religion any more important than Zoroastrianism, Manichaeism, or any of the other unpronounceable *-ism's* from the ancient world? The answer is yes. Gnosticism is extremely important to establishing trust in the Bible.

Gnosticism often comes up in discussions about the Bible because the Gnostic gospels include many striking similarities to the canonical Gospels. The Gnostic gospels include figures such as Thomas, Judas, and Jesus. There are references to the Sermon on the Mount, the Last Supper, and the resurrection of Jesus in these Gnostic texts. These similarities have led scholars to allege that Gnosticism was actually the earliest form of Christianity. The argument typically goes like this: Gnostic communities were in fact legitimate Christian communities attempting to faithfully live according to the teachings of Jesus. They wrote texts that they used for catechesis and worship just like every other Christian community. Unfortunately, a small group of churches and leaders came against these communities and maliciously deemed them unorthodox and heretical. Therefore, what we call Gnosticism is in fact a legitimate and valid depiction of the teachings of Jesus. The New Testament texts in the Bible today are there only as a result of political maneuvering and power plays. The Gnostic texts actually capture the true beliefs of the Early Church and give us a better picture of Jesus than the canonical Gospels in the Bible. . . .

Hit the brakes! There are serious problems with this argumentation. And these problems begin with the two most basic facets of Gnosticism: rejection of the material world and salvation through secret knowledge. These two beliefs are entirely antithetical to the foundational beliefs of Judaism found in the Old Testament. (Remember, Jesus was Jewish and He held to the teachings of the Old Testament.) These Gnostic gospels are a sharp departure from the established Old Testament teachings. Genesis makes it clear that God created the world with good intentions and declared it to be very good (1:31). Scripture gives no indication that the material world is inherently bad and the spiritual world is inherently good; rather, Scripture depicts a good creation turned bad as a result of sin. The spiritual realm is broken by sin just as the material realm is broken by sin. And God has promised to redeem both the spiritual and the material realms. The Old Testament Scriptures cannot be squared with Gnosticism on this core belief.

Second, the Old Testament does not support a belief in secret knowledge leading to salvation. There are numerous instances of exactly the opposite: God does not hide from the nations. The work of God is put on display for all people to witness. The Word of God is proclaimed for all people to hear. Secret knowledge, hidden wisdom, and private enlightenment are nowhere to be found in the Old Testament. Salvation is not a hidden truth to be uncovered by the individual; salvation is from God, openly shared with the nations, and freely given for all to receive.

Secret knowledge, hidden wisdom, and private enlightenment are nowhere to be found in the Old Testament.

There are many questions still surrounding Gnosticism. Yet, one thing is overwhelmingly clear: Gnosticism was not an early form of Christianity. There is no way that the Gnostic texts could have presented a legitimate form of Christianity since they fundamentally opposed the core teachings of the Old Testament. Gnosticism was never Christian. It is a different religion with different texts and different beliefs.

STUDY QUESTIONS

CHAPTER 5

1. What is the appeal to claiming there are "secret books" that were excluded from the Bible?

2. Why is the account of Serapion of Antioch helpful in seeing how the Early Church sorted through which texts to use?

3. The Early Church used different categories for classifying texts when deciding whether they should be included in the biblical canon or not. What were these different categories?

4. The canon was not determined by putting books on an altar and waiting for some to fall down. Could God have directed the formation of the canon even if it did not happen miraculously?

5. What are some ancient nonbiblical texts that offer a depiction of Jesus?

6. Who were some influential Early Church writers defending the faith from false teaching?

7. How is Gnosticism fundamentally different from Christianity?

6

OLD AND OBSOLETE

Floppy disks used to be considered cutting-edge technology. Cassette tapes were once a revolutionary feat of modern invention. Access to the Internet was at one time confined to large desktop computers with connection to a landline. In ancient times (circa AD 1990), people used to receive notifications on devices known as "pagers" and then respond to the message with something known as a "public pay phone." These historic artifacts are difficult to find anymore because they are old and obsolete. It is hard to find a public pay phone anywhere because smartphones have long since replaced this antiquated technology. It is even harder to find a floppy disk because modern computers no longer support that form of memory storage. Some of you reading this may not even know what a floppy disk is!

The Bible is often lumped into the same category as floppy disks, pagers, and public pay phones. People will readily admit that the Bible was once timely and relevant; previous generations received it as important and influential. Today, however, the Bible is like an old iron lung once used for treating polio—an interesting artifact that previous generations relied on to cure their ailments. Many people argue that the Bible should now be relegated to the museum. They argue that the Bible is so old and obsolete that it cannot possibly speak to people today. Contemporary culture claims that the time of biblical relevancy has come and gone. History and literature classes now read the Bible alongside Ovid's *Metamorphoses* or Tacitus's *Agricola*. Older generations might still read Scripture, but younger generations read something else.

To liken the Bible to iron lungs, floppy disks, and dial-up Internet is to misunderstand and misjudge the nature of Scripture. The Bible is God's Word. It is timeless, eternal, and still speaks powerfully today. The Bible is permanently relevant. It was relevant when it was first composed. It has been relevant to every subsequent generation. And it will remain relevant for every generation to come. The Bible, as the cradle of Christ delivering salvation and eternal life to its hearers, will never become old and obsolete. Jesus is always relevant and therefore the Bible is always relevant. Jesus will never go out of style and thus Scripture will never go out of style. His words are always opportune and will always speak to contemporary society. And that means the words of Scripture are always opportune and will always speak to contemporary society.

The Bible is permanently relevant.

CLAIM:
SCRIPTURE IS TOTALLY OBSOLETE BECAUSE IT IS FROM AN ANCIENT AND PRESCIENTIFIC SOCIETY.

This is a haughty claim abounding in modern arrogance. Making this sort of argument implies that the knowledge of previous generations ought to be dismissed simply on the grounds of being ancient and prescientific; the past offers little value and no society before the scientific revolution (sixteenth century) possessed any sort of trustworthy knowledge. This is dismissive, overconfident, and rude.

This claim is predicated on the notion that modern society knows better than any ancient society. The assumption is that people today have a better view of knowledge than any other generation. Modern thinkers claim to see further, know more, and think clearer than anybody else in human history, because they learned from the great thinkers who came before them. This attitude is often described as "standing on the shoulders of giants." The insight and ignorance, discoveries and disasters of all previous generations provide an ideal vantage point for present knowledge; these are the giants on which modern thinkers stand. Therefore, this assumes that modern people are on the highest rung of human knowledge. Standing at the edge of human history and looking out over all previous generations automatically means that modern society knows best.

There is one serious flaw with this line of thinking: assuming that the giants are facing in the right direction. It is quite possible that the knowledge of previous generations has modern society facing the wrong way, assuming the wrong assumptions, and thinking erroneous thoughts. There are many examples of giants facing in the wrong direction: Charles Darwin (1809–82), certainly a giant in the field of natural history, proposed the notion of natural selection as a vehicle for evolution. His well-known tenant of "survival of the fittest" was the foundation for many future thinkers, namely Thomas Henry Huxley (1825–95). Known as "Darwin's Bulldog," Huxley stood on the shoulders of his intellectual predecessor and fought hard for the widespread acceptance of natural selection. Standing on the shoulders of Thomas Henry Huxley was a grandson named Julian Huxley (1887–1975). Drawing on the work of previous generations, Huxley applied natural selection to humans in the study of eugenics. Huxley was a prominent member of the British Eugenics Society, which sought to eradicate inferior races and classes of people. Standing on the shoulders of giants, Huxley saw forced sterilization, withholding basic medical treatment, and strict limits on procreation as the best way to improve society. Exterminating minorities and poor people was deemed good, right, and salutatory. Clearly, he was standing on the shoulders of giants facing in the wrong direction. It is important to choose wisely which giants you stand on.

There are countless other examples like that of Darwin, Huxley, and Huxley. The point is that modern thinkers do not know best simply because they have the advantage of inheriting the knowledge of previous generations. Modern people can be just as wrong as ancient people. Contemporary thinkers can be just as misguided as classical thinkers. Determining truth is not as simple as rejecting the old and embracing the new. Dismissing the Bible as obsolete simply because it is ancient and from a prescientific society is foolish.

Assuming that the Bible contains nothing more than ancient words about ancient events is incorrect. The Bible certainly contains the past work and words of God. Yet, the Bible is more than that. It is God speaking in the present. The Bible is not an echo of what God once spoke long, long ago. Rather, it is God shouting into the hearts and ears of people today. The Bible is God shouting into your heart and into your ears. Scripture is far more than an account of divine work in the distant past; it is a head-on collision between sinners and the mercy of God here and now. Encountering the Word of God means encountering the active love and work of Jesus Christ in the present.

The message of the Bible is special and unlike anything else in all of creation. It does not grow old or obsolete, because it is God daily and actively speaking into your life. It is important to understand how the message of the Bible is unlike any other message. Distinguishing between general revelation and special revelation reveals that the Bible cannot ever be deemed old or obsolete:

General Revelation: There are countless texts, works of art, and natural features in creation that can reveal something about the nature of God. Texts about moral virtues can reveal something about God's will for creation: Aesop's Fables illustrate how lying is wrong. Old cautionary tales argue on the basis of natural law that taking the possessions of others leads to greater trouble. The ancient Code of Hammurabi suggests the innate human desire for justice. Works of art can reveal something about the beauty that God has woven into creation: Vincent Van Gogh's magnificent painting *The Starry Night* (1889) captures a glimpse of the heavens declaring the handiwork of God. Pablo Picasso's abstract painting *Guernica* (1937) reveals something of God's disdain for death. Natural features in creation are evidence of the existence of God: The deep depths of the Mariana Trench stretching miles underwater testify to the depths of God's creative powers. The rocky peaks of Yosemite National Park loom high and mighty in the horizon, whispering the presence of an even higher and mightier God.

These are all types of *general revelation*, revealing something about the nature and work of God. This sort of revelation is described in Scripture: "The heavens declare the glory of God, and the sky above proclaims His handiwork" (Psalm 19:1). Nevertheless, the messages conveyed by these types of general revelation lack specificity and detail. It can be ascertained from general revelation that justice is good, yet the exact contours and confines of God's specific will for justice remain unclear. It is clearly evident from Shakespeare's *Romeo and Juliet* that sacrifice is a powerful act of love, yet God's perfect plan of salvation through the sacrifice of Jesus Christ is not evident in this text. General revelation is silent when it comes to revealing God's plan of salvation.

Special Revelation: Unlike general revelation, *special revelation* is God's direct revelation spoken to His creation. God's speaking to Moses in the burning bush (Exodus 3) is an example of special revelation; Moses could not have ever known the name of God apart from it being revealed to him through this special revelation. God's speaking through the mouth of prophets (Jeremiah 1:9; Isaiah 20:2) is another example; if it had not been revealed by God through the prophets, Israel would not have had knowledge of a coming Messiah born into the house of David. In the New Testament, God's direct revelation came through the preaching and teaching of Jesus. Special revelation about God's plan of salvation in Christ Jesus could not be known apart from the revelation of God. Jesus Christ—God in human flesh—had to reveal God to His people. Furthermore, special revelation also came through the inspiration of the Holy Spirit writing through the authors of the New Testament texts; John would not have had knowledge of God's future plans as described in Revelation if it had not been specially revealed to him.

Unlike the general revelation of God woven into the tapestry of creation (Romans 1:20), special revelation contains knowledge of salvation that could not possibly be known apart from God's direct revelation (Romans 10:14). The Bible is God's special revelation to His creation. The Bible imparts knowledge of salvation that could not possibly be discovered elsewhere. The Bible is God's special revelation and therefore it cannot ever become old and obsolete. Works of general revelation may become old and obsolete; cautionary tales may resonate with one generation yet be deemed old and obsolete by later generations. God's special revelation, on the other hand, continues to speak to each and every subsequent generation. As long as sin separates people from God, the Bible will always be timely and relevant. As long as death destroys life, the special revelation contained in Scripture will continue to speak loud and clear. As long as the devil is determined to undermine the kingdom of God, the Gospel of Jesus Christ will be a sweet, sweet sound to sinners.

The Bible is God's special revelation to His creation.

The Gospel refuses to be considered an old and obsolete relic of the past. The word *Gospel* comes from the Greek word (*evangelion*) for "good news." There is a good reason that the Gospel is good news. Something is regarded as news if it is an event that happened in a specific time and place. News is different from an opinion or advice because it relies on events in a specific time and place. News always occurs within the existing context of a place; news of a military victory makes sense only within the preexisting context of political strife. And news always shapes the future of a place; news of a drought ending leads to widespread rejoicing and hope for a better tomorrow. The life, death, and resurrection of Jesus Christ is good news because it was the action of God within a specific time and place.

And the Gospel is still good news today. The Gospel of Jesus Christ is proclaimed into the preexisting context of your life. The life, death, and resurrection of Jesus is spoken into your past foibles and failures, sins and shortcomings, death and despair. The Gospel is news of a loving and gracious God acting on your behalf, redeeming you for all eternity, and making all things new. The good news of Jesus entirely reshapes your past, present, and future. Past sins are covered in the blood of Jesus. Present fears are emptied of their power by the empty tomb. Future life is proclaimed by the sure and certain promise of God. This good news will never grow old or become obsolete.

WHAT YOU NEED TO KNOW

Modern people can be just as wrong as ancient people. Contemporary thinkers can be just as misguided as classical thinkers. Dismissing the Bible as obsolete simply on the grounds of it being ancient and from a prescientific society is wrong because it misunderstands the nature of Scripture. The Bible imparts knowledge of salvation that could not possibly be discovered elsewhere. It is God shouting the Good News of Jesus into your heart and ears. As long as sin separates people from God, the Bible will never become old or obsolete. As long as death destroys life, the special revelation contained in Scripture will continue to speak loud and clear. God's Word proclaims Christ into the lives of His people and is therefore fully ancient yet forever relevant.

CLAIM:

THE BIBLE IS SO OLD THAT IT COULD NOT POSSIBLY SPEAK TO CONTEMPORARY CULTURE.

The more things change, the more they stay the same. According to Ecclesiastes, "What has been is what will be, and what has been done is what will be done, and there is nothing new under the sun" (1:9). Don't believe it? Here are some instances of there being nothing new under the sun:

- Ancient Greek physicians and philosophers, such as Hippocrates and Aristotle, wrote about the struggles of acne. They proposed treatments for pimples that relied on sulfur, honey, and other peculiar remedies. This means that teenagers in Athens probably spent way too long in the bathroom examining zits, washing their faces, and lathering up with sulfur and honey. The very same ailment that plagued ancient teenagers continues to strike the youth of today. Acne has caused every generation of adolescents under the sun to be self-conscious and embarrassed.

- Way back in about AD 397, Augustine of Hippo wrote about making up stories to impress his friends. In his spiritual autobiography entitled *Confessions*, Augustine wrote about his time studying rhetoric in Carthage between the ages of sixteen and nineteen. He would hear his classmates tell stories about their sexual encounters with women, every subsequent story attempting to outdo the other. Having no real experiences of his own, Augustine simply made up stories about hooking up with the young women of Carthage. Locker rooms today are no different from locker rooms in North Africa during the fourth century.

There is nothing new under the sun. Acne and locker rooms are just a few of the ways that ancient history is hardly different from present-day culture. Much of daily life in antiquity is conversant with daily life today.

Although the Bible is an ancient text—with many writings extending long before the time of Aristotle, Hippocrates, and Augustine—it has extremely timely and relevant verses. There are a number of verses in Scripture that people identify as speaking loud and clear to contemporary culture today. These verses are well known by many people and highlighted as particularly relevant because their inspirational words convey timeless wisdom:

- "Love is patient and kind; love does not envy or boast; it is not arrogant or rude. It does not insist on its own way; it is not irritable or resentful; it does not rejoice at wrongdoing, but rejoices with the truth. Love bears all things, believes all things, hopes all things, endures all things" (1 Corinthians 13:4–7).

- "Therefore do not be anxious about tomorrow, for tomorrow will be anxious for itself. Sufficient for the day is its own trouble" (Matthew 6:34).

- "For everything there is a season, and a time for every matter under heaven" (Ecclesiastes 3:1).

As long as people have love in their hearts, fear for tomorrow, and a longing to make sense of the ever-passing present moment, then these verses of the Bible will speak to contemporary culture. These verses are standards when it comes to greeting cards, wedding readings, and social media posts. Whether people know the Bible or not, they are often familiar with these verses.

Nevertheless, there are more than just a couple of verses in the Bible that still speak to contemporary culture. It is not as though a small portion of Scripture is relevant to contemporary culture while the bulk of it is outmoded, outdated, and out of style. The entire Bible—every chapter, every verse, and every word—speaks loud and clear to contemporary culture. Even the most arcane sections of Scripture are timely and true today, tomorrow, and forever.

The Bible is relentlessly relevant since it is God's speaking in the ever-present moment. It is God's ancient Word in the past and it is God's present proclamation today. It is what God said long ago and it is what God says to you right now. There is no point in going through the Bible and highlighting only the relevant verses because you would end up highlighting the entire thing. God's Word destroys sin, delivers life, and declares the precious name of Jesus Christ. This will never go out of style. The Bible is eternally relevant as it constantly speaks God's commandments and promises, the Law and the Gospel:

God's Word destroys sin, delivers life, and declares the precious name of Jesus Christ. This will never go out of style.

Law: The Bible contains God's clear instructions for holy living. There is no uncertainty about God's will for how you are to live your life because it is clearly articulated by God's Word. You do not need to look into your heart or up at the stars to determine what is right; you simply need to look to what God has declared to be right. There are numerous examples of God speaking commandments to His people:

- "You shall love the LORD your God with all your heart and with all your soul and with all your might" (Deuteronomy 6:5).

- "He has told you, O man, what is good; and what does the Lord require of you but to do justice, and to love kindness, and to walk humbly with your God?" (Micah 6:8).

The Bible reveals God's standard for truth, righteousness, and justice. This is not a temporary truth or a regional standard for righteousness. God's commandments are the standard for right and wrong stretching in the past, speaking in the present moment, and spreading indefinitely into the future. The Holy Spirit utilizes the Law to curb evil impulses, show sinners where they have erred, and guide people in holy living. No matter how long ago these commandments were first spoken, they are spoken anew by the Holy Spirit in your life. The Law incessantly speaks divine truth into hearts of falsehood. It has always and will always shine a spotlight on the darkness of sin.

This means that the Law is eternally relevant to your life. As long as you have a penchant for sin, you will need the Law of God. Hearing God's standard for holiness prepares your heart for mercy, carving repentance out of stony sin. When you dishonor your parents by disregarding their concerns, God's commandment to honor your mother and father shows you the waywardness of your actions. When you begin to gossip about a friend, God's commandment against bearing false witness stops you before the slanderous poison drips from your tongue. God's standard for holiness is not relegated to ancient history; it is alive in your life and reveals how your actions align with God's will.

Gospel: The Bible is not merely a handbook for holy living. The Bible is the proclamation of the Gospel of Jesus Christ. God speaks hope into your ear and salvation into your heart. God sings new songs of joy into the dirge that is your past. Scripture declares God's unending promises to you. The Law reveals your sinfulness and makes clear your need for a Savior. The Gospel reveals that your Savior has come in Christ Jesus.

While the Bible contains God's commandments for holy living, it also contains God's good promises for you:

- "For the Son of Man came to seek and to save the lost" (Luke 19:10).

- "I am the good shepherd. The good shepherd lays down His life for the sheep" (John 10:11).

- "For God so loved the world, that He gave His only Son, that whoever believes in Him should not perish but have eternal life" (John 3:16).

- "But God shows His love for us in that while we were still sinners, Christ died for us" (Romans 5:8).

To be certain, the Gospel of Jesus Christ is ancient. God spoke a word of promise to Adam and Eve in wake of their rebellion: "I will put enmity between you and the woman, and between your offspring and her offspring; He shall bruise your head, and you shall bruise His heel" (Genesis 3:15). God refused to speak only curses on His fallen creation; rather, He spoke a bold and living promise into the death and decay of a fallen world. This promise of God made to Adam and Eve is known as the *Protoevangelium*. Proclaimed at the very beginning of the Bible, this was the first mention of a coming Messiah sent by God to redeem a broken creation. Thousands of years have passed since God proclaimed His first promise to creation. The Gospel is certainly ancient.

Yet it is never obsolete.

This ancient Gospel is full of present power. These old words of promise speak new words of life today. Salvation through Christ Jesus was spoken long ago. And it speaks to you here and now. The birth of an ancient Savior in faraway Bethlehem offers present peace in the midst of your closest troubles. The perfect life of Jesus way back in history delivers perfect holiness to you right now through faith. The distant death of Jesus on the cross at Calvary comes near to you in the hearing of God's Word. The power of the empty tomb over two thousand years ago has the power to leave your tomb empty; death has been defeated. None of this is a passing fad or a fleeting phenomenon. The ancient Gospel of Jesus Christ contains present power for this very moment:

Despair. Contemporary culture struggles with profound despair. Nihilism is a philosophical ideology claiming that life is essentially without meaning, purpose, or value. This belief in a meaningless existence has resulted in a culture of despair. What is the meaning of human life if it is nothing more than a random assemblage of chemicals, confusion, and chance? What is the point of anything if the planet Earth is just a chunk of rock floating in an infinitely tiny part of the universe? Contemporary culture suffers from the despair that comes from imbibing a steady dose of atheism, nihilism, and pessimism. Into this meaningless mind-set, the Gospel proclaims God's eternal purpose and plan for salvation. Life has eternal value; Scripture clearly states that God values life so highly that He is willing to do anything—anything!—even shed His own blood in order to redeem life from the clutches of death. Life has eternal purpose; the Bible clearly conveys God's plans that human creatures are to live in community and harmony with the rest of creation and with Him. The Bible is a powerful antidote to the despair of contemporary culture: "Through Him we have also obtained access by faith into this grace in which we stand, and we rejoice in hope of the glory of God" (Romans 5:2).

Sickness. Long ago, people suffered from sickness and disease. Today, people still suffer from sickness and disease. Despite all of the advances in medicine, there is still the constant threat that cancer, diabetes, miscarriages, and infertility will bring an end to life. The common cold, broken bones, and indigestion have afflicted people for thousands of years and they will afflict people for another thousand years. Human bodies break down, shut down, and let down. The Bible speaks a strong word into the sickness that is so prevalent in our world today. Scripture proclaims that God has fearfully and wonderfully made human bodies, that Jesus is the Great Physician capable of healing bodies and souls, and that the Holy Spirit reveals wisdom and truth to earthly doctors and nurses. The Bible speaks of God's power to form living creatures out of dust and bone (Genesis 2:7, 21), of Jesus' power to heal broken bodies with mud and spit (John 9:6–7), and of the Holy Spirit's power to restore life to lifeless bodies (Romans 8:9–11). The Bible proclaims the eternal health of the Divine Physician to a world full of sickness.

Evil. Contemporary culture denies the existence of God and the authority of Scripture. Nevertheless, people today readily agree that evil exists in the world. Terrorism, racially motivated violence, and widespread genocide provide proof of the reality of evil. It is not hard to find someone willing to admit the presence of evil. It is hard, however, to find someone with an adequate response to the problem of evil. Governments have attempted to stop evil yet have succeeded only in waging endless wars. Schools strive to develop productive citizens yet have become a target for shootings. Doctors try to mitigate evil with medicine, hoping that troubled individuals take their pills and not hurt anyone. Far better than anything else in contemporary society, Scripture offers a truly honest assessment of evil and depicts a comprehensive response. Unlike many other religious texts, the Bible actually takes evil seriously. It depicts the profound depravity of a fallen creation and tells how God will not rest until evil is adequately vanquished. God does not respond to evil with legislation, education, or medication; God responds to evil by giving His own life on the cross. God came into a world of evil in order to heal a world of evil. The Bible speaks to the problem of evil by proclaiming the life, death, and resurrection of Jesus: "But the Lord is faithful. He will establish you and guard you against the evil one" (2 Thessalonians 3:3).

Death. As with all the previous issues, contemporary culture has no adequate response to death. Death has plagued all people, in all places, at all times; the grave does not discriminate between young and old, rich and poor, powerful and destitute. The grave has no racial boundaries. All people are all subject to the power of death. It is a perennial problem for which contemporary culture has no permanent solution. Contemporary culture simply does not know what to do with death. The most popular response is denial: refuse to have funerals, conceal lifeless bodies in a casket, and pretend that a loved one has not died. Others prefer to handle death through endless distractions; rather than consider mortality, people keep so busy that they never have to ponder their own perishability. Instead of stopping to attend a wake, contemporary culture spends all of its wakeful hours distracted by work and play, amusement and diversions.

Scripture has much to say to contemporary culture on the topic of death. The Bible does not deny death. Rather than pretending it is not an issue, God's Word is a head-on confrontation with death. It does not try to avoid death with euphemisms; there is absolutely no mention in the Bible of people becoming angels on clouds and playing harps after they die. Nor is there the fanciful thinking that life after death is endless golf courses, all-you-can-eat buffets, and your own personal paradise. The Bible does not succumb to the hopelessness of contemporary culture; Scripture refuses to depict death as a hopeless inevitability in which the deceased are no more than the newest layer of sod. God's Word depicts death as an unnatural aberration within God's creation. God witnessed the horror of death, promised to remedy this pain, and came into the world to conquer death. The Bible reveals how God put death to death through the cross and the empty tomb of Jesus Christ. Throughout the Gospels, Jesus interrupts funerals by raising the dead back to new life. Through faith in Him, God promises to interrupt your death when He raises you to new life: "'O death, where is your victory? O death, where is your sting?' The sting of death is sin, and the power of sin is the law. But thanks be to God, who gives us the victory through our Lord Jesus Christ" (1 Corinthians 15:55–57).

WHAT YOU NEED TO KNOW

There is nothing new under the sun. Daily life in antiquity is not really that different compared to daily life today; teenagers have always suffered from acne and fear of not fitting in with their peers. Although the Bible is especially old, that alone is not reason to reject it as obsolete.

The Bible speaks loud and clear to contemporary culture today. However, it is not as though only a few verses of the Bible still speak to contemporary culture and the rest are irrelevant. The entire Bible—every chapter, every verse, and every word—speaks boldly to the world today. The Bible is relentlessly relevant because it is God's speaking in the ever-present moment, proclaiming divine commandments and promises through Law and Gospel. The Law curbs evil impulses, shows sinners where they have erred, and guides people in holy living. The Gospel reveals that your Savior has come in Christ Jesus. These ancient words are full of present power.

The Gospel was spoken long ago. And the Gospel still speaks to you here and now: "The promise is for you and your children and for all who are far off, everyone whom the Lord our God calls to Himself" (Acts 2:39). The birth of a Savior long ago in a faraway place offers you near and present peace in your deepest despair. The ancient death and resurrection of Jesus gives new life now and forever. The power of an empty tomb and some neatly folded burial garments—though left empty thousands of years ago—will leave your tomb empty one day. None of this is obsolete. It is full of present power and future hope.

Cautionary Tales

Cautionary tales are an effective way of scaring kids into compliance. This subgenre of folklore depicts warnings to children in a narrative form. Each story begins with a disobedient child refusing to heed a warning from a responsible adult or animal. Rather than minding this sage advice, the careless child continues with the bad behavior. The story then concludes when the act of defiance leads to a gruesome demise. Despite their horrific conclusions, adults share these cautionary tales with children. (Usually, these stories are told just before the kids go to bed. . . . Sweet dreams!)

One of the most popular books of cautionary tales is *Der Struwwelpeter*, a German children's book written by Heinrich Hoffmann in 1845. It was at one time a wildly popular children's book throughout Europe, translated into several different languages, and reprinted in multiple editions. Hoffmann wrote the book for children ages 3 to 6. Complete with rhymes and illustrations, this book depicts wayward children meeting untimely deaths or horrific punishments.

"The Story of Cruel Frederick" depicts a young boy who is mean to animals; he rips the wings off flies and throws kittens down the stairs. Eventually, a dog by the name of Tray bites Frederick for his bad behavior. The dog bite becomes infected and forces Frederick to be bedridden. The story ends with Tray eating Frederick's soup and pudding in front of him while laughing maniacally. The story of a dog biting children and then eating their food is surely enough to keep young children and even some adults awake at night. Fear not. . . . There are plenty more gruesome cautionary tales in this once popular children's book!

"The Dreadful Story of Pauline and the Matches" is a tale of a little girl named Pauline. She is left alone at home while her mother and nurse go to run some errands. Finding some matches on the table, Pauline decides to light them and watch how pretty they are. The cat warns her that she will burn to death if she plays with matches; yet, Pauline disregards this fearful feline. The tale ends with Pauline catching fire and the cats frantically trying to meow for help. The final scene of this cautionary tale depicts the cats crying over a pile of ashes. (You can connect the dots yourself.)

"The Story of Little Suck-a-Thumb" is a delightful warning against thumb-sucking. The tale depicts a boy named Conrad. His mother warns him against sucking his thumb and tells him that, if he continues to do so, a roving tailor will come and cut of his thumbs. Conrad disregards this warning and pops a thumb in his mouth. Alas! The roving tailor comes out of nowhere and cuts off Conrad's thumbs with a few snips. And, to make things even worse, Conrad shows his mother what happened and she tells him that she is not at all surprised.

That's enough for now.

There is something important to recognize in these caution-ary tales: they are old and obsolete. A teacher would be fired for reading these cautionary tales to young children today. Child protective services might want to investigate a family who uses these cautionary tales as bedtime reading. These tales for children are shocking and disturbing by modern standards.

And they are less than two hundred years old. Let that sink in for a moment. Only a few generations ago, these cautionary tales were considered essential reading for young children. Parents were remiss if they missed out on the opportunity to educate their children through these fearful stories. However, today these cautionary tales are flatly rejected as psychologically abusive.

Compare this with the Bible. Scripture is thousands of years old, and it has resisted becoming obsolete. God's Word continues to speak good news, convey wisdom, and proclaim eternal truth. The entire Bible speaks boldly to contemporary culture. Not just some of it. Not just a chapter here or a verse there. The whole Bible is relentlessly relevant because it is God's speaking in the ever-present moment. Scripture proclaims God's will for His people in the Law. God's Word makes sinners aware of their waywardness and curbs their evil impulses. And Scripture proclaims the Gospel. God's Word reveals that your Savior has come in Christ Jesus to forgive all your sins and give you eternal life.

It took less than two hundred years for Heinrich Hoffmann's cautionary tales to go from widely accepted to wildly inappropriate. In over two thousand years, the Bible is still relevant today. The Bible contains the truth of salvation that could not possibly be discovered elsewhere. It speaks the Good News of Jesus into your life. The Bible will never become obsolete because it contains words of truth, life, and hope in a world of falsehood, death, and despair.

CHAPTER 6

1. What texts do people rightfully regard as old and obsolete?

2. What are some examples of modern thinkers being misguided in their thinking?

3. Read Romans 1:19–20. Are these words of Paul an example of general revelation or special revelation?

4. Read Matthew 28:18–20. Are these words of Jesus an example of general revelation or special revelation?

5. What is required in order for something to be considered "news"?

6. Why is the good news of Jesus Christ rightly considered "news"?

7. The Bible speaks loud and clear to contemporary culture. How is the Bible speaking loud and clear in your life lately?

7

TRANSLATED AND TAINTED

The game of telephone is a classic. Children gather in a circle, and the game begins with one person whispering a message to another: "The cat has a fluffy tail." This message is then transmitted from person to person around the circle until it gets back to the first person. Without fail, the original message always ends up twisted, transformed, and tainted: "The bat ate a puffy snail."

Why does it always happen this way? People. A message traveling from ear to brain and then from brain to mouth is often transformed. If one person hears the message incorrectly, then the original content is totally lost. If someone decides to go rogue and swap out the original message with her own message, then the entire group is now subject to this distorted message. If the message going around the circle becomes utter confusion, then some well-meaning individual might try to correct it by inserting a new word or thought. Regardless of exactly how the message becomes tainted, it is always the flawed work of people trying to communicate.

A common claim against the Bible is that it is a massive game of telephone extending across many miles and millennia, translators and transcribers. If a childish game on the playground with only six players inevitably goes awry, then how much worse would it be if you had thousands of people and many generations? Scripture is accused of being translated and tainted as it passed from person to person. Skeptics argue that translating the Bible into other languages radically transforms the original message. Others try to claim that it is not the translating that taints the text as much as it is personal interpretation; trying to read and understand the Bible results in an infinite number of different interpretations. It does not matter how closely the translation reflects the original message, because individuals will just interpret the Bible to meet their own agendas. These are just a few of the claims made against Scripture suggesting that it is horrendously translated and tainted.

The truth is that the Bible has greater precision of translation and interpretation than any other book. Period.

Both ancient and modern translations of the Bible exhibit tremendous care for maintaining the integrity of the text. Generations of biblical scholars have devoted their entire academic careers to developing best practices for translating the Bible into different languages and faithfully interpreting the text. Translating the Bible into another language is not haphazard guesswork; the work of translation is based on an established methodology, public accountability, and rigorous scholarly standards. Interpreting the Bible is far from asking the question "What do you think this means?" Rather, a well-established subdiscipline known as hermeneutics is committed to properly interpreting Scripture. Translation and interpretation of the Bible is not a huge game of telephone. It is a thoroughly academic study with generations of established best practices.

In fact, the rigorous scholarship of biblical translation and interpretation is so solid that nonbiblical scholars rely heavily on the knowledge of biblical scholars. Properly translating and interpreting the Bible has profoundly shaped how other scholars work with nonbiblical texts. Researchers working with historic works of literature—whether it is translating a text from one language to another or preparing an original manuscript for modern publication—must rely on the work of biblical scholars. The excursus at the end of this chapter will explore this in greater detail. It is abundantly obvious that neither translation nor interpretation leave the Bible twisted, trifled, or tainted.

CLAIM:

TRANSLATIONS OF THE BIBLE ARE EXTREMELY DIFFERENT FROM THE ORIGINAL TEXTS.

There is a Latin expression about translating texts, *omnis traductor traditor*, that means "every translation is a traitor." In other words, the act of translating a text from one language into another betrays the original. Something is inevitably lost in translation—a word may not have an exact counterpart, an idiom may not work quite right, or the sound of the text may be changed. The act of translating a text from one language to another is a betrayal of the original work.

How much betrayal are we talking? Does translating a text from Hebrew to Spanish require striking down the first word in every sentence? Is going from Greek to English an assassination of the text likened to Brutus knifing Julius Caesar? Not really. Saying that translations of the Bible are extremely different from the original text demonstrates an inexperienced knowledge of translations. The betrayal that happens when translating a text from one language to another is not wanton disregard for the integrity of the message; translators agonize over crafting the best translation. Rather, the notion of translations being traitors recognizes how a certain *je ne sais quoi* is missing in translations. (Saying "I don't know what" would not fully capture the idea of an intangible and indescribable quality the same way that the French expression *je ne sais quoi* does. It is almost as if the English translation betrays the French. Hmm. . . .)

Suppose that you are at the theater in the front row viewing a production of Shakespeare's *Othello*. Your vantage point allows you to see details that may be lost to others. You see beads of sweat rolling down Othello's forehead and pooling up on his brow. You see sprays of spit mist in the air as Iago shouts his lines. The stems of the cherries on Desdemona's handkerchief are clearly distinguishable. You see the plot unfold, hear the iambic pentameter in the spoken lines, and weep at the final scene; yet, you also notice the tiny details, such as laces on the actor's shoes, theater assistants standing right off stage, and the guy next to you texting on his phone.

After the final curtain, you prepare to leave the theater. As you are walking out, you notice they are selling video copies of the production you just watched. You purchase one and go home.

Watching the production on video is different. Although they were filming the exact same play you just watched, you notice that the camera angles allow for a different perspective. There are times in the video when the camera zooms in and pans out. There are moments when the camera operator chose to focus on Desdemona rather than Othello. Certain distractions—the people offstage and the guy texting—are missing from the production on video. The experience of watching the production in person is markedly different compared to watching the production on video.

Despite the differences in the live and recorded versions, the two are still overwhelmingly similar. It is not as if one is a tragedy and the other is a comedy. Othello does not die in the live version and remain alive in the video version. The characters are all the same. The dialogue, costumes, and plot remain identical in both versions. The differences are greatly eclipsed by the similarities.

This example depicts the relationship between the original text of the Bible and the many different translations. There are certainly differences between Scripture in the original languages and the many different translations. All translations are in some way traitors to the original text. Nevertheless, this in no way substantiates the claim that translations of the Bible are totally different from the original texts. Most translations of the Bible aim to faithfully and accurately deliver the original text into a different language. Just as the video recording of a play attempts to faithfully capture the live production, translating the Old Testament from Hebrew and Aramaic into Farsi attempts to faithfully capture the original text. The difference between the original text and the translated text are on the same level as the differences between a live production and the video recording of the same play.

What exactly are the differences between translations of the Bible and the original texts? Before discussing that question, it is important to know something about the methodology that guides translators in their work. The methodology used by a translator has a strong influence on the final translation.

Functional Equivalence: This methodology attempts to make the translation function in the target language as the original did in the source language. According to this methodology, translators aim to preserve the *thought* of the text in the translation. This means that wording may be slightly changed in order to capture the meaning of the original text. For instance, the Hebrew language describes anger with the expression "his nose burned" (see Genesis 30:2; Exodus 4:14; Numbers 22:22). A functional equivalence for this expression would be to simply use the word *angry* or *furious*. This, however, requires translators to deviate slightly from the original wording in order to make the translation clearer. The goal with this methodology is clear reading and understanding over literal and rigid translation of the original text. This is often described as thought-for-thought translation rather than word-for-word translation. It makes for especially readable and easily understood translations. Examples of translations that rely heavily on functional equivalence include the Contemporary English Version and the Good News Bible.

The downside to this methodology is that the translators must make interpretational decisions on behalf of the reader. It is certainly true that all translations require a translator to make interpretational decisions on behalf of the reader; however, these decisions can be more prominent in functional equivalence translations. Attempting to capture the message of the text means that a translator must read the text, decide what he or she thinks is the intended message of that text, and then craft a translation that conveys this message. Translators using the functional equivalence methodology sometimes make significant decisions for readers. This is problematic because the reader of the translation is unaware that these decisions have been made.

Formal Correspondence: This methodology attempts to create a correspondence between the words in the source language and the target language. This is a word-for-word translation rather than a thought-for-thought translation. If the text suggests that someone's "nose burned," even if it is obvious that this means the person was angry, a strict formal equivalence translation would translate this literally so that it corresponds to the original text. Rather than making the decision on behalf of the reader, translators using this methodology aim to convey the words of the original text in the translated text. Decisions are based on closely reflecting the original. This makes for a translation that very closely mirrors the original. Examples of formal correspondence translations include the English Standard Version, New American Standard Bible, and the Amplified Bible.

The downside to this methodology is that clarity and readability can suffer in the translations. Since the Bible is an ancient text, there are many unique expressions and idioms that can be confusing to modern readers. An extremely literal translation of an ancient text can make for quite confounding reading. Even though the translation is a word-for-word copy of the original text, the wording and sentence structure can be so foreign that it is difficult to understand.

Paraphrase: Paraphrases of the Bible—also known as an idiomatic translation—attempt to make the text as readable and understandable as possible. Although all translations attempt to make the text readable and understandable, some translations make large interpretive glosses in the process. This is effectively rewriting the biblical text. Paraphrases make large departures from the original text for the sake of readability. Therefore, an idiomatic translation will not match up sentence-to-sentence with the original text. Instead, a whole paragraph or chapter will be paraphrased to facilitate reader comprehension. The benefit to these sorts of translations is that they read like any other modern text; reading an idiomatic translation of the Bible is as easy as reading the newspaper. Examples of these include The Message and The Living Bible.

The drawback is obviously the huge departures from the original text. Usually paraphrases are the work of a single author rather than an editorial committee. This does not automatically mean that idiomatic translations are completely troublesome and tainted; however, paraphrasing the Bible results in a greater distance between the original text and the reader. The original text is chopped up and prepared in an extremely specific way according to an individual's theological disposition. Rather than being just the Word of God, paraphrases are the Word of God as told by someone else.

It is important to note that all English translations of the Bible use a combination of functional equivalence, formal correspondence, and paraphrasing. All of these are utilized in serious Bible translations. However, it is clear that some translations rely on one methodology more than the other. Some translations rely on both functional equivalence and formal correspondence equally. Therefore, it is helpful to put translations on a spectrum in order to see how heavily a methodology is utilized.

This overview on translation methodologies shows that there is no deception when it comes to Bible translations. Just as a scientist clearly reports her research methodology in the published report, Bible translators clearly report their methodology used for translation. There is no deception as to whether a translation aims to be a word-for-word translation of the original (formal correspondence), a thought-for-thought translation of the original (functional equivalence), or a paraphrase of the original. This is almost always clarified in the explanatory notes of the translation. Furthermore, many modern Bible translations will reveal the names and affiliations of the translators and editorial committee. This lets readers know who worked on the project and what theological predispositions these translators might have brought to bear on the text. Savvy readers can use this information to choose a Bible translation that more faithfully reflects the original text.

God's Word is not limited to just one language or translation. It is not as if God's Word can be rightly heard only in Greek or Hebrew. Furthermore, there is not just one single translation of the Bible that contains God's Word. The Word of God can transcend different languages and translations.

WHAT YOU NEED TO KNOW

Translations are traitors. It is true. A translation must in some way betray the original text. Certain expressions may not come through in a new language, the exact wording or sound of a text may be slightly distorted, and something in the original will always be lost in the translation. Nevertheless, the degree to which translations are traitors is negligible. It can be compared to the differences between a live production and a video recording. The original text in the original languages and the translation of the original text both reveal the exact same Jesus Christ. In the original Greek New Testament manuscripts, Jesus dies on the cross, is buried in the tomb, and is resurrected to new life. In an Arabic translation of the New Testament, Jesus dies on the cross, is buried in the tomb, and is resurrected to new life. God's Word was written in Hebrew, Aramaic, and Greek. And God's Word can be translated into Farsi and French, Creole and Cantonese.

Translators use certain methodologies when translating a text from the original language to a different language. But the translation methodology used to create a translation is clearly disclosed, as are the actual translators working on the project. Similar to a scientist disclosing the research methodology along with the names of the researchers on a project, Bible translations make it all public for people to know. Rejecting the Bible as being translated and tainted is the same as rejecting scientific research projects. Scientists utilize a certain research methodology in order to translate raw data into usable results; Bible translators utilize a certain methodology in order to translate raw manuscripts into usable translations. Neither good scientists nor good translators hide the methodology behind their work.

The degree to which translations of the Bible deviate from the original texts is negligible. The extremely precise and transparent work of translation means that the Bible can be trusted even in a different language.

CLAIM:

Cancel culture

Woke culture

EVEN CHRISTIANS DISAGREE ABOUT HOW TO INTERPRET THE BIBLE. WHY SHOULD I TRUST IT IF YOU CAN'T EVEN AGREE AMONG YOURSELVES?

If that is true, then you should probably set this book down right now. Rejecting the Bible on the basis of differing interpretations would require you to reject every book ever written. And every work of art ever produced. And every movie ever made. And every musical composition ever arranged. And just about everything else in the world.

All these works—the Bible, works of literature, paintings, sculptures, musical scores and arrangements, movies, and theatrical productions—are subject to different interpretations. Two people watching a film will have two different interpretations of what is meant by the cinematography. Two people reading T. S. Eliot will have two different interpretations of *The Waste Land*. Two different people listening to John Coltrane will have different interpretations of the meaning behind *A Love Supreme*. Unless you are ready to reject movies, literature, music, and just about everything else, then you probably should not reject the Bible on the basis of differing interpretations. If you do not want to reject all these things, then you should probably learn something about hermeneutics.

The theory and methodology of interpretation is known as hermeneutics. The goal of hermeneutics is to answer the question "What does this mean?" Hermeneutics is not relegated only to the Bible; rather, many nonbiblical scholars use these techniques to inform their work. Shakespearean scholars must not only read but also interpret his works. Scientists read and interpret the results of scientific research. Politicians read and interpret polls and determine how voters are responding to certain policy decisions. These are all examples of hermeneutics in action.

Although hermeneutics is used in many different disciplines, scholars studying the Bible were foundational in developing this academic practice. Methods for interpretation were first formulated through reading, discussing, and applying Scripture. For as long as the Bible has existed, people have been developing best practices to help interpret these sacred texts. An ancient Jewish text known as the Midrash is an example of the long-established practice of hermeneutics. The Midrash is a commentary on the Old Testament describing best practices of interpreting the meaning of various words, sections, and books within the Hebrew Scriptures. With the formation of the New Testament canon, the Early Church discussed hermeneutics extensively and developed numerous principles for interpretation. This continued through the Middle Ages, into the Reformation, and to the present day. When you read the Bible and seek to understand the meaning of the text, you are engaging in a centuries-old effort to interpret God's Word. You are not the first person nor are you the last person to interpret the Bible.

Interpretation is a communal practice. Readers of the Bible, whether they are aware of it or not, are constantly drawing on the influences and assumptions of other people. These influences and assumptions arise within interpretive communities such as denominations and congregations, universities and scholarly circles. Every interpretive community has a set of assumptions about the nature of a text and how it ought to be understood. Some communities read the Bible as the inspired and inerrant Word of God written through human authors. Other communities read the Bible as a purely human work of literature no different from *Moby Dick* or the phone book. Yet other communities read the Bible as containing divinely inspired truths hidden amid the debris of human thoughts. These radically different assumptions about the nature of Scripture direct how these communities interpret the text. If a community approaches Scripture as the Word of God, then its interpretation will be directed by that assumption. If readers approach Scripture as merely good literature, then their hermeneutical practice will reflect that belief. If an interpretive community begins with the assumption that the Bible is harmful to society, then this notion will dictate which tools readers use to interpret the text. The assumptions held by a community have a great influence on how they interpret the Bible.

OPERATING SYSTEMS FOR INTERPRETATION

Biblical interpretation can be divided into two different categories: historical-critical and historical-grammatical. Think of these as different operating systems for a computer. The operating system for a computer determines how a user logs on, navigates through programs, and performs tasks. The overall user experience depends on the operating system. The same holds true for these two methods of biblical interpretation.

Historical-Critical Method: This method of interpretation assumes that the Bible is a purely human text and the aim of interpretation should be to understand the historical factors that gave rise to the writing. This treats the Bible like any other work of literature. The methodology scholars use to interpret *The Great Gatsby* is similar to the methodology for interpreting Scripture. Examining the decadence of the Roaring Twenties, the persistent alcoholism of F. Scott Fitzgerald, and the influence of the book's editor is an essential key to understanding *The Great Gatsby*. Examining the brutality of the ancient Near Eastern culture, the sacred rituals of ancient tribes, and potential influences of later editors is supposedly the key to understanding Scripture according to this method. The goal is to deconstruct the text and reveal what is hidden behind it (i.e., author, historical setting, and political forces). The historical-critical method relies only on tools developed by historians, anthropologists, sociologists, and literary scholars.

There are two substantial problems with this method of interpretation. First, since the historical-critical method aims to deconstruct the text and reveal the hidden factors behind the text, this method obliterates the text and leaves only shreds of Scripture for readers to interpret. Take the words of 1 Peter 3:3 as an example: "Do not let your adorning be external—the braiding of hair and the putting on of gold jewelry, or the clothing you wear." The historical-critical method would explore why the author might have written this text. Standard questions for interpretation would be to ask why Peter focuses on women, what personal and cultural factors led to Peter writing this text, and what other historical examples of male dominance are similar to this writing. Scholars may look to the scant references to Peter's marriage and speculate why only his mother-in-law is mentioned and not his wife (Matthew 8:14). It may be concluded that Peter had a relationship with his wife that was either not worth mentioning or perhaps even deeply conflicted. Therefore, the interpretation of this text is that Peter targets women with the words of 1 Peter 3:3 because he has a troubled relationship with women in his own life. The takeaway for modern readers of this verse: do not be chauvinistic. (Seriously, this is how some scholars use the historical-critical method.)

The other problem with this approach to interpreting Scripture is denying that it is the Word of God. This method assumes that the Bible is a purely human text like the phone book or a handbook on tax code. This is problematic because the Bible asserts that it is the Word of God on numerous occasions (Deuteronomy 9:10; 2 Chronicles 34:31; Acts 18:11; 2 Timothy 3:16; 1 Thessalonians 2:13). It is overwhelmingly clear that the Bible was both written and received as God's

Word conveyed through human authors. The historical-critical method reverses this and approaches it as strictly human words claiming to be divine. Although the authors and original readers would disagree, modern scholars argue that the Bible is exclusively the word of man. This would be like a modern scholar claiming that Sophocles was wrong in thinking that *Oedipus Rex* was a tragedy; although the author of the play would disagree, the story is actually a comedy and not a tragedy. This so-called scholar would be laughed out of every lecture hall and classroom. Yet, scholars using the historical-critical method consistently reclassify Scripture despite the clear objection of the authors and original readers.

Historical-Grammatical Method: This method of interpretation strives to accurately understand the author's original meaning for the text. According to this method, the goal of biblical interpretation is to draw on reputable scholarship—history, archaeology, and ancient languages—in order to determine the meaning of the text as the original author and audience would have intended. Rather than trying to deconstruct a text to determine the historical factors that gave rise to the writing, the historical-grammatical method aims to understand what the text meant in its original setting. Scholars use a number of techniques in order to determine the original meaning of the text.

Exegesis is the practice of closely studying the language, syntax, and grammar of a text. Understanding the original language is vital to accurately understanding a text's original meaning. Words function in different ways depending on historical context and literary context. The meaning of a word can change and evolve over time (the word *awful* once meant awe-inspiring yet now describes a dreadful situation). Similarly, a word can mean something quite different based on where it is located in relation to other words. (For instance, in the sentences "Run as fast as you can!" and "The publisher did a large print run," the word *run* means two different things.) Exegesis relies on reputable scholarship in order to ascertain how words and sentences were understood in their original setting.

Genre is another important factor for biblical interpretation. A genre is a literary category or type of writing. Scripture is comprised of many different genres: narrative, poetry, prophecy, parables, apocalyptic writing, along with other subgenres. These genres are essential to understanding how to interpret the text. A poem relies on figurative language in a way that historical narrative does not. Apocalyptic writing reveals a glimpse into the future while a parable is an earthly story depicting a heavenly truth.

Context, like genre, is crucial in understanding the meaning of a text. Context is the text surrounding a text: the sentences, paragraphs, and chapters surrounding the text that is to be analyzed. Biblical interpretation relies on the surrounding chapters and books of the Bible in order to gain an understanding of a text. In order to understand a sentence in Genesis, it is vital to understand how it relates to surrounding sentences, other books in the Pentateuch, and the Bible as a whole. This allows Scripture to interpret Scripture.

Fighting for a faithful reading of Scripture, orthodox interpretations of the text, and accurate applications into daily life is worth the struggle.

Like the historical-critical method, the historical-grammatical method relies on reputable scholarship to inform interpretation. Nevertheless, there is one major distinction between these methods: the historical-grammatical method interprets the Bible with the recognition that it is the Word of God. It relies on human scholarship insofar as the Bible is God's Word composed through human authors within a historical context. It relies on faith given by the Holy Spirit insofar as the Bible is the eternal Word of God. Rather than treating Scripture as merely text, this method recognizes the Bible as divinely inspired.

FIGHT THE GOOD FIGHT

Arguing that the Bible should not be trusted because of the multitude of different interpretations misses a serious point: the truth is worth a fight. The apostle Paul used the image of a boxer fighting in a match when he said, "Fight the good fight of the faith" (1 Timothy 6:12). Fighting for a faithful reading of Scripture, orthodox interpretations of the text, and accurate applications into daily life is worth the struggle. The disagreements about how best to interpret the Bible are not evidence that it should not be trusted; rather, they are proof that Christians take the Word of God seriously. God's Word is precious and captivates the undivided attention of God's people. Shrugging our shoulders, looking the other way, and refusing to care when people claim an outlandish interpretation of the Bible is not an option. Doing that would undervalue, undermine, and undercut God's Word.

Divergent interpretations are not always bad. Take the phone book as an example. One person might interpret the phone book as being good for starting a campfire. Someone else might interpret the phone book as useful for elevating short drivers. Another person may interpret the phone book as a way to determine if old friends are still in the area. And it is possible that another person might even use the phone book to look up phone numbers. (I know that might be hard to believe.) This panoply of interpretations is not a problem. You can sleep at night knowing that there are different interpretations about how best to use the phone book. This diversity of creative perspectives is rather refreshing.

Divergent interpretations can also be rather bad. Take a research report on cardiac surgery for example. One heart surgeon may interpret the text as indicating that the best practice is to take your heart out and sell it on the black market. Another heart surgeon might understand the report as suggesting that your heart be replaced with a paper cutout of a heart. And yet another heart surgeon may read the report and interpret its words as the scientifically verified, widely confirmed best practices for heart surgery. Which one do you want performing your heart surgery?

Wildly divergent interpretations of Scripture are eternally dangerous. Having your own particular interpretation of the Bible may seem like a harmless expression of individuality. Seeking new and inventive ways to understand Scripture may appear to be a good practice. Nevertheless, these divergent interpretations can be as dangerous as misinterpreting how to perform heart surgery. Reading the Bible and interpreting Jesus to be a human teacher on the level of Buddha and Steve Jobs is eternally dangerous. Understanding the Gospel to be merely an encouragement to live a good life has unending consequences. Incorrectly interpreting the creation of the world, the gravity of sin, the incarnation of Jesus, and the reality of the resurrection will have tragic results. These are foundational truths that are worth a fight.

Diverging interpretations of Scripture have always threatened the truth. And God's people have always fought the fight of rightly interpreting God's Word. During His earthly ministry, Jesus constantly confronted wrong interpretations of Scripture. The Early Church tirelessly fought to maintain a faithful interpretation of the Bible. Martin Luther spoke up when he witnessed the Gospel of Jesus Christ being misinterpreted in the Scriptures. It is never good to fight simply for the sake of argumentation. Nor is it good to fight for matters that are frivolous (known in theology as *adiaphora*). It is wrong to fight just for the satisfaction of being right.

It is right, however, to fight for a faithful interpretation of Scripture. Struggling to maintain an orthodox reading of the Bible does not undermine its trustworthiness. It does just the opposite. Striving to have a faithful interpretation of God's Word—even if that leads to disagreements—is essential to trusting the Bible. The Bible is trustworthy because generations of believers have been guided by the Holy Spirit to struggle with their hearts and minds for an ever-faithful interpretation of God's Word.

WHY SHOULD I TRUST THE BIBLE?

WHAT YOU NEED TO KNOW

Rejecting the Bible on the basis of differing interpretations would require you to reject every book, poem, painting, symphony, and just about everything else ever composed. Rather than rejecting the Bible on account of differing interpretations, it is important for the reader to know something about hermeneutics. Developed as a result of biblical scholars reading Scripture—yet now widely used by other academic disciplines—hermeneutics seeks to determine the meaning of a text. There are two main operating systems for biblical interpretation: the historical-critical method and the historical-grammatical method. The historical-critical method assumes that the Bible is a purely human text and that the aim of interpretation should be to understand the historical factors that gave rise to the writing. The historical-grammatical method strives to accurately understand the author's original meaning for the text. Whereas the historical-critical method treats the Bible as a purely human book, the historical-grammatical method recognizes that it is God's Word composed through human authors. These different methods result in substantially different interpretations of the Bible.

Some interpretations matter more than others. It makes no difference if you incorrectly interpret the phone book. It makes an earthly difference if your heart surgeon rightly interprets surgical protocol. And it makes an eternal difference in heaven and earth if you rightly interpret God's Word. Struggling to get the right and faithful reading of the Bible is worth the fight. The Holy Spirit employs our hearts and minds, academic scholarship and the communal deliberation of the Church to maintain a faithful interpretation of God's Word.

William Faulkner

The word *translate* derives from Latin and means "a carrying across" or "a bringing across." Translating often entails carrying a text across different languages—carrying a text from Italian to Swahili, French to English, or Mandarin to Arabic. The work of a translator is to bring communication from a source language to a target language.

Translation, however, is not limited to carrying texts across different languages. Preparing a handwritten manuscript for print publication is a form of translation. Editors must decipher the author's handwriting and margin notes, scribbles and corrections in order to establish a final copy. Carrying a text from the original handwritten source—known as a holograph—to a printable copy is tantamount to translation. Without proper care and attention to detail, the translated version can betray the original work.

William Faulkner, illustrious American author and central figure of the Southern Renaissance, left a bounty of handwritten holographs for editors to translate. He left handwritten holographs for every novel from *The Sound and the Fury* (1929) to *The Hamlet* (1940). However, due to his illegible handwriting that even he himself could not decipher, Faulkner then began composing his works on a typewriter. (That might give you an indicator of how difficult it is to translate his handwritten manuscripts.) Faulkner's extant papers included thousands of pages of handwritten manuscripts, typescripts, corrected and uncorrected proofs for publication, notes, drafts, revisions, and outlines. This trove of material is housed in a number of libraries and private collections.

This massive collection of handwritten copies and working drafts is certainly a great gift to the literary community. The thousands of scribbled pages reveal the composition process of a meticulous writer. Nevertheless, these thousands of handwritten pages fraught with edits and notes present a serious frustration to modern publishers attempting to establish a printable copy. Translating the piles of holographs left behind by Faulkner is harder than translating Shakespeare into Swahili.

The difficulty for modern publishers is trying to establish a single print copy from all the rough drafts, edits, and revisions. Faulkner was meticulous in his composition. He would write and then heavily revise his work: individual words or entire phrases were crossed out, phrases or paragraphs were moved from one place on the page to another, and sometimes an entire section would be rearranged within the manuscript. There are instances in which a portion of text is scissored from one section and glued into another section of the manuscript. This flurry of revisions makes it difficult to determine which edits were made when and by whom. Did Faulkner himself make the edit or was this made at the request of an editor or someone else? There are many instances in which the

interaction between author and editors is clear; however, there are many others in which it is difficult to trace the changes made to a novel as it went from Faulkner's hand, through various revisions, and finally to the published text.

Modern publishers could simply reproduce Faulkner's novels from one of the printed editions. It would be far easier to merely copy a first edition of the text rather than going back to the holographs. Indeed, it would certainly be easier, but it would definitely not be better. Copying the printed editions of Faulkner's work is the same as copying a copy; any mistakes made in the copy would be included in the reproduced text. The only way to ensure that Faulkner's original writing is preserved is to go back to the sources—the piles of handwritten manuscripts—and perform the work of carefully translating them into a printable copy. And this is exactly what Faulkner scholars do today. Experts pore over the manuscripts, debate handwriting and margin notes, examine context, and establish a publishable translation based on

Faulkner's handwritten manuscripts. Scholars then have to justify their decisions and provide evidence for their work so that other scholars can examine the final copy.

The work of translating William Faulkner is quite similar to translating the Bible. Rather than relying on a copy of a copy, biblical scholars go back to the sources. These sources include thousands of handwritten manuscripts that often contain margin notes. Biblical scholars preparing a translation must pore over these manuscripts, debate the handwriting, examine the context, and establish a printable translation of Scripture. Translators of the Bible must also justify their decisions and provide evidence for their work to other biblical scholars.

It is important to recognize the similarities between translating Faulkner and translating the Bible. Just as modern literary scholars trust the work of translation in establishing modern copies of Faulkner's writing, modern readers of the Bible can trust the work of translation in establishing copies of Scripture. Imagine a high school student refusing to read *As I Lay Dying* because she does not trust that the copy accurately depicts the original text. Do you think the teacher would give her a pass on the assignment because the copy in her hand is not exactly the same as the original text penned by Faulkner? Certainly not! The teacher would explain how experts carried the text from handwritten copy to printed form and that the text in her hands can be trusted.

Scholars of Faulkner have been translating his work for less than a hundred years. Scholars of the Bible have been translating God's Word for thousands of years. The methods that scholars use to translate *As I Lay Dying* rely on the methods established by scholars translating the Bible. If translations of Faulkner can be trusted, then the translations of the Bible can be trusted even more.

CHAPTER 7

1. How much of a difference is there between translations of the Bible and the original text?

2. Have you ever seen a live production of a play you first saw on video? What were the differences between the productions?

3. How is reading a translation of the Bible similar to viewing a video recording of a play?

4. What are the three different methodologies that guide Bible translators in their work?

5. The United States Constitution is an important document. What are some different interpretations of this text?

6. Interpretation is a communal practice. How have you seen this statement in action?

7. Why is it a "good fight" to defend the Bible from wildly divergent interpretations?

8

BIGOTED AND BIASED

Old encyclopedias make some rather peculiar claims. Polio was at one time described as an incurable epidemic trouncing around the globe and threating the well-being of children. The Cold War was once characterized as a hotly contested battle between democracy and communism with the imminent fear of a missile attack. The substance and structure of the moon was at one time described as unknown and *probably* not made of cheese. Old encyclopedias even once described certain races of people as genetically and intellectually inferior.

These texts are outdated, outmoded, and out-and-out wrong. A vaccine has offered a cure for polio. The Iron Curtain is now more like docile drapes. The moon is definitely not made of cheese (bummer). The notion that some races are intrinsically superior to others has been debunked, deconstructed, and dismissed. Certain ethnicities are not innately stronger, smarter, or more equipped than other ethnicities to be leaders. People are people regardless of their skin color, language, or ethnicity. There is no legitimate basis for promoting one ethnicity over another.

Old encyclopedias, since they are filled with obsolete knowledge, have little purpose today. Certainly these old texts are interesting from a historical standpoint; they provide a glimpse into what people once thought about the world. These texts are valuable for nostalgic reasons; Grandma once paid a ton of money to purchase a set of encyclopedias, and she guarded them with her life. Nevertheless, old encyclopedias have lost their value as an authoritative text that can speak accurate knowledge into the present day.

The Bible is wrongly classified when it is equated with an old encyclopedia. Claiming that the Bible is bunk because it is racist and sexist is a deeply flawed argument. There are numerous instances in the Bible that prove God's Word is neither racist nor sexist. It is overwhelmingly clear that Scripture is a proclamation of God's love for all people. Not just some people. Not just these people. Not just men. All people.

To be certain—there is no doubt that the Bible has been wrongly used to substantiate racist and sexist ideologies. People have plucked texts out of context as a pretext for hate. Many have tried to use Scripture as a way to legitimize slavery and inequality, abuse and violence. Hateful people have attempted to cut and paste God's Word to support their own bigoted human words. These practices misuse, misappropriate, and entirely misunderstand the Bible.

Wrongly using the Bible for hate does not render it untrustworthy. Using a seatbelt incorrectly does not mean that the seatbelt failed; rather, the person using the seatbelt failed to use it correctly. It is wrong to argue that a seatbelt cannot be trusted if you never put it on correctly in the first place. It is not the seatbelt that failed; it is the person using the seatbelt who failed. The Bible does not fail when people use it for hateful purposes; the people using the Bible for hate have failed to use it correctly. If you read Scripture and understand it to say that some people are more valuable to God than others, then you are doing it wrong.

CLAIM:

THE BIBLE IS RACIST AND PROMOTES SLAVERY.

Some of the claims I address in this book are outlandish and silly. Some of these claims hardly deserve to be addressed. Not this one. This claim is discussed with good reason. Countless people have used the Bible to promote racism and slavery. Throughout history, numerous people have used the Word of God to prop up their own hateful words. This is tragic.

The Bible, however, does not advocate racism or slavery. Using God's Word in this way is using it incorrectly. Simply because the Bible speaks about slavery does not mean that it advocates slavery. It is especially important to understand the distinction between description and prescription. Understanding this distinction correctly will ensure that Scripture is not misappropriated to support racism or slavery.

Description: This means simply describing a person, situation, or occurrence as it happened. An example of this in the Bible is when Abram asks Sarai to tell people that she is his sister rather than his wife (Genesis 12:10–13). This passage is simply describing what Abram did out of fear. This is not an example of the Bible making lying normative or permissible. Anyone citing this text as an example of Scripture permitting lying is wrong. Describing someone lying is not the same as authorizing someone to lie. Another example of the Bible functioning descriptively is when Abram and Sarai resolve to have a child through Hagar (Genesis 16:3). This is a description of what occurred and should not be misunderstood as permitting polygamy.

Likewise, the Bible describing racism and slavery is not the same as authorizing racism or slavery. An example of this in the Bible comes from Philemon. The apostle Paul describes Onesimus as a slave or bondservant (Philemon 16). This is not prescribing slavery as normative or acceptable. Instead, this is simply describing the situation as it happened: Paul was in prison when he met a runaway slave named Onesimus. This text is not advocating slavery just as it is not advocating the imprisonment of Christian missionaries. The Epistle to Philemon discusses slavery insofar as it is necessary to describe an actual event that occurred in the Early Church. It is vitally important to recognize when the Bible is functioning descriptively.

Prescription: There are many other times in which the Bible functions prescriptively. Rather than simply describing something that occurred, the Bible prescribes a certain course of action. The Bible may *de*scribe Abram lying about Sarai being his wife, but the Bible *pre*scribes truthfulness (Leviticus 19:11; Matthew 5:37; Ephesians 4:25). These texts are not merely describing what occurred; rather, these are prescribing God's people to speak truth.

Another example of this can be seen in the Epistle to Philemon. The apostle Paul gives prescriptive words to Philemon in regard to his runaway slave: "So if you consider me your partner, receive him as you would receive me" (Philemon 17). Paul is prescribing the mercy of Jesus over the bondage of slavery. He is calling for Philemon to remove the shackles of slavery and receive Onesimus as a brother in Christ Jesus. A specific course of action is prescribed: cancel the enslavement of Onesimus.

It is important to recognize when the Bible is functioning descriptively and when it is functioning prescriptively. Without this recognition, one is likely to falsely accuse Scripture of being racist. Opponents of the Bible read description as prescription; they find sections of the Bible describing racial inequality and claim it is advocating this practice. For instance, the Book of 2 Chronicles provides a historical description of Solomon's rule:

> All the people who were left of the Hittites, the Amorites, the Perizzites, the Hivites, and the Jebusites, who were not of Israel, from their descendants who were left after them in the land, whom the people of Israel had

not destroyed—these Solomon drafted as forced labor, and so they are to this day. (8:7–8)

This describes Solomon's administrative decisions in dealing with people of other nationalities; that is not the same as prescribing this course of action as normative for all leaders. The fact that Solomon's actions are included in the biblical narrative does not make them permissible. This is not prescriptive discourse.

FOR ALL PEOPLE

There are many occasions where the Bible prescribes racial unity. God's Word boldly calls for neighborly love regardless of your neighbor's skin color. Scripture does not vacillate, equivocate, or speculate on whether God values people of different ethnicities: God loves all people no matter where they come from, what food they eat, or what language they speak. There are many instances in the Bible where God calls for a radical valuation of all people. There are way too many to include here. However, there are some particular verses that should be highlighted:

- Isaiah 56:1–8—These verses call for radical multiethnic inclusivity. God does not reject people on the basis of skin color, ethnic background, or nationality. The kingdom of God is not segregated: "For My house shall be called a house of prayer for all people" (v. 7). Modern recipients of these words welcome this multiethnic inclusivity and expect that God would not be racist. Ancient recipients of these words, however, would have found them downright scandalous. Racism was rampant in antiquity. It was a widespread practice in the ancient Near East to subjugate anyone of a different ethnicity, enslave other races of people, and exclude them from full standing in the community. Spoken into a culture of systemic racism, these words of Isaiah would have been countercultural. Inviting the nations to call on the name of Yahweh in prayer and participate in worship would have been revolutionary. While others were advocating slavery, imprisonment, and genocide on the basis of ethnicity, God's Word provided a clarion call to welcome the nations.

- Mark 16:15—After His death and resurrection, Jesus sent the disciples out with clear instructions: "Go into all the world and proclaim the gospel to the whole creation." Notice what Jesus did not tell the disciples. Jesus did not instruct the disciples to share the Gospel only with people of the same race, language, or ethnicity. There was no racial limit placed on the Good News of Jesus. It was not just for Jews, Judeans, or people just like the disciples. It was not limited to the people of Galilee, Gaza, or Gaulanitis. The Gospel is for all people. Jesus sent the disciples out into the whole creation with the message of eternal salvation. He sent them to the Roman Empire—a society where one-fifth of the population was enslaved—with the message of God's free mercy for all people. If it was scandalous for Isaiah to proclaim God's desire for a house of prayer for all nations, then it was doubly scandalous for the Jewish Messiah to open the gates of heaven to all people.

- Galatians 3:28—The apostle Paul proclaimed clear words of multiethnic inclusivity to the Early Church. He wrote his Letter to the Galatians largely as a response to ethnic tensions that came as a result of a faction known as "Judaizers." This faction of Jewish Christians claimed that the Gentile followers of Jesus had to conform fully to Jewish practices (circumcision and kosher eating) in order to be part of the Church. Paul sets the record straight by proclaiming, "You are all one in Christ Jesus." The powerful love of Jesus that transcends human traditions, ethnic boundaries, and skin color is able to unite disparate communities. Despite the differences in tradition, ethnicity, and gender, believers have something far greater in common: salvation through faith in Christ Jesus. This does not destroy the unique aspects of ethnicity and gender; instead, it allows us to celebrate our differences from a place of unity in Christ Jesus. Fear, jealousy, and hate are nailed to the cross. Our hearts of stone filled with racism, xenophobia, and ethnocentrism have been put to death and buried in the tomb of Jesus. His resurrection swallowed up sin and death for all people regardless of race.

In the midst of rampant racism, the Bible resounds with a clear message of God's love for all people. There is no question that the message of Scripture transcends language, ethnicity, culture, and skin color. The Bible does not advocate bigotry on the basis of race. Anyone using Scripture to promote racism is misappropriating, misunderstanding, and misusing God's Word.

RACE AND RELIGION

What about all the sections of the Bible that appear to be openly promoting racism? Good question. There is no denying the fact that, at times, Scripture seems to herald hegemony, celebrate colonialism, and reinforce racism.

The distinction between race and religion is hard to untangle throughout history. It was rather common in antiquity for race and religion to be conceived of as one and the same: Individuals residing in the land of Canaan predominantly worshiped Baal and Marduk. The nearly universal veneration of Ra, the god of the sun, immediately came to mind when ancient people thought of Egypt. Greek citizens were expected to worship the gods of the Greek pantheon. It was common in antiquity to lump together nations and notions of religion, races and rituals, people and practices of belief. Radical individualism—where belonging to a group of people ethnically does not mean belonging to that group of people religiously—is a modern invention. The notion of distinguishing race and religion would be a foreign concept in antiquity.

Nevertheless, there is a clear difference between race and religion, ethnicity and eternal truth. God loves all races. God is open to all ethnicities. God welcomes every tribe and nation to be part of the kingdom of God. This does not mean, however, that the Bible remains silent when it comes to the worship of false gods and goddesses. God's Word speaks out against false gods of wood and stone, gems and gold. Scripture says something about wrong beliefs and behaviors: God is not open to the worship of idols.

When the Bible addresses idolatry, it often takes the shape of addressing a specific nation or group of people. This can sound like racism to modern ears:

- "Behold, the LORD is riding on a swift cloud and comes to Egypt; and the idols of Egypt will tremble at His presence, and the heart of the Egyptians will melt within them. And I will stir up Egyptians against Egyptians, and they will fight, each against another and each against his neighbor, city against city, kingdom against kingdom" (Isaiah 19:1–2).

- "While Israel lived in Shittim, the people began to whore with the daughters of Moab. These invited the people to the sacrifices of their gods, and the people ate and bowed down to their gods" (Numbers 25:1–2).

- "Did not Solomon king of Israel sin on account of such women? Among the many nations there was no king like him, and he was beloved by his God, and God made him king over all Israel. Nevertheless, foreign women made even him to sin. Shall we then listen to you and do all this great evil and act treacherously against our God by marrying foreign women?" (Nehemiah 13:26–27).

People have used these verses to claim that the Bible is xenophobic, nationalistic, and entirely opposed to interracial marriage. Using these verses as a proof text to argue that the Bible is against interracial marriage is a serious misappropriation. Notice that the issue with the Israelites marrying people of other nations is that they then accepted false gods. Union with other people led to union with other gods. Scripture is warning against accepting the idols of other nations. These are just a few examples of the rather subtle distinction between race and religion.

IS THE BIBLE PRO-SLAVERY?

Yes, the Bible is pro-slavery. However, it is entirely not in the way you would think. The Bible is 100 percent against earthly slavery: sex slavery, forced labor, sweatshops, and abusive working conditions. Spaniard colonizers were entirely wrong to use the Bible in the sixteenth century as a basis for subjugating inhabitants of Mesoamerica. Britain and America horribly misappropriated God's Word when they used it to substantiate the enslavement of African natives in the seventeenth and eighteenth centuries. And anybody trying to use the Bible to validate abusive working conditions today is simply wrong.

Scripture does, however, say this about slavery: "But thanks be to God, that you who were once slaves of sin have become obedient from the heart to the standard of teaching to which you were committed, and, having been set free from sin, have become slaves of righteousness" (Romans 6:17–18). Faith in Christ Jesus makes you a slave to Him (1 Corinthians 7:21–23). Previously enslaved to sin and death, Jesus purchased you at the expense of His blood shed on the cross. You have been bought with the steep price of the life, death, and resurrection of Jesus Christ (1 Corinthians 6:20).

Jesus spoke on this matter as well. He described all people as being slaves to sin (John 8:34). Jesus encouraged the disciples to make themselves as slaves to all people: "But whoever would be great among you must be your servant, and whoever would be first among you must be slave of all" (Mark 10:43–44). And then Jesus goes even further to describe His own life as a life of servitude to others: "For even the Son of Man came not to be served but to serve, and to give His life as a ransom for many" (Mark 10:45).

In this sense, the Bible is pro-slavery. Nevertheless, the servitude that the Bible advocates is not racial, hateful, or abusive. The servitude of Jesus is nothing like the slavery of antebellum America, child labor in the diamond industry, or sex-slavery of young women. Scripture ultimately advocates being set free from the shackles of sin and death and being purchased with the precious blood of Jesus. Once enslaved to sin, you are now property of Christ Jesus. And that is an extremely good thing.

Scripture advocates being set free from sin and purchased by the blood of Jesus. This is clearly a spiritual enslavement to sin and a divine form of redemption. Does this mean that the Bible is pro-slavery in an earthly sense? No.

The Bible makes it clear that Jesus is making all things new (Revelation 21:5). This new creation began with Christ's death on the cross and the empty tomb. Creation is not the same place as a result of the life, death, and resurrection of Jesus. Faith in Christ Jesus means that all people are radically united in Him and awaiting the new creation. The Church is the vanguard of the new creation as a public witness to the new life in Christ. Nevertheless, the Church lives with one foot still in the old creation, which is laced with sin, death, and the devil. The Church is an outpost of the new creation dwelling within the old creation. Therefore, Scripture offers guidance to God's people on how to live as the new creation of Christ living in the old creation of sin: "Bondservants, obey your earthly masters with fear and trembling, with a sincere heart, as you would Christ. . . . Masters, do the same to them, and stop your threatening, knowing that He who is both their Master and yours is in heaven, and that there is no partiality with Him" (Ephesians 6:5, 9).

166

This can appear to be an approval of slavery, but the point here is not to uphold the inequality between bondservants and masters, slaves and overlords. Rather, the point here and elsewhere in the New Testament is to give guidance to the new creation of Christ living in the old creation of sin. It is also important to recognize that the servitude described in the New Testament was nothing like the slavery of antebellum America; it was far more like the modern relationship between employer and employee. Teachers, accountants, and physicians in the Roman Empire were often slaves. Though not always the case, many servants in the Roman Empire had a relatively high degree of personal agency.

WHAT YOU NEED TO KNOW

Describing racism and slavery is not the same as endorsing racism and slavery. Scripture makes it overwhelmingly clear that God's love extends to all nations, languages, and ethnicities. God desires His house to be a house of prayer for all people. Not just some people. Not just people who eat certain food, speak a certain language, or come from a certain place. God has forever abolished racism and slavery in Christ Jesus. The life, death, and resurrection of Jesus Christ has ushered in a new creation that is free from sin and slavery, racism and racial inequality: "There is neither Jew nor Greek, there is neither slave nor free, there is no male and female, for you are all one in Christ Jesus" (Galatians 3:28). This does not, however, mean that God is open to false beliefs and humanly constructed idols. Scripture calls out nations enslaved to false gods and idols. This can sound like xenophobia when it is simply truth calling out deception. Similarly, the Bible makes references that sound as if it is endorsing slavery. This is not the case. These are simply words of guidance for how to live as a new-creation people in the old creation.

The only sort of slavery the Bible endorses is slavery to Christ's righteousness. God was not content knowing that you were enslaved to sin, death, and the devil. Therefore, God's Word makes it exceptionally clear that you have been bought at an exceptionally high price with the precious blood of Jesus. This is true for you. And this is true for all people.

CLAIM:

THE BIBLE IS CLEARLY BIASED TOWARD MEN. IT WAS WRITTEN BY MEN AND IS PRIMARILY FOR MEN.

There is no denying the fact that the Bible was disproportionately written by men. This much of the claim is accurate. Claiming that since men wrote the Bible it is only for men, however, is entirely inaccurate. As the previous section discusses, God's Word is for all people regardless of race or gender. There is no validity to the notion that since men composed the Bible, it is primarily for men. Claiming that the Bible is not also for women is completely illegitimate and an easily refuted claim.

Just because handrails have a bias for right-handed people does not mean that left-handed people cannot also use them. (I say this as a left-handed person living in a right-handed world.) Just because astronauts drink tangy orange juice in space does not mean that earth-dwelling civilians cannot also drink it for breakfast. Just because computer scientists created the Internet as a durable communication network in the event of nuclear fallout does not mean that teenagers cannot use it to share selfies. Simply because God used men to compose the Bible does not mean that it disregards women.

Although the majority of the books of the Bible bear the names of men, that does not mean that God's Word excludes women. Scripture abounds with radically influential women: Eve, Sarah, Rebekah, Leah, Rachel, Miriam, Deborah, Hannah, Esther, Ruth, Anna, Elizabeth, Mary, and Lydia. This list hardly begins to cover the many women in the Bible. Many of the most important promises in Scripture rely on women:

Protoevangelium—The *Protoevangelium* is the first mention of the Gospel made in Scripture. And this promise centers on a woman: "I will put enmity between you and the woman, and between your offspring and her offspring; He shall bruise your head, and you shall bruise His heel" (Genesis 3:15). Following the rebellion of Adam and Eve, God distributed curses to the serpent. As God cursed the serpent with a lowly existence, He also promised that his days were numbered. This promise of God is made especially early in the Bible and it hinges on a woman giving birth to a child that will destroy the serpent. The salvation of God's fallen creation hinges on a woman.

Progenitor—The mother of a nation is often known as a *progenitor*. God immediately began the work of fulfilling His promise made in the Garden of Eden by making nations. Through Eve, God populated the whole earth and began the process of making good on His promise of bringing forth a Savior from a woman. The Book of Genesis gives special attention to the matriarchs in the family tree of this promised Savior. God promised that Sarah would give birth to Isaac: "The LORD visited Sarah as He had said, and the LORD did to Sarah as He had promised" (Genesis 21:1). God made another central promise to Rebekah when He told her that she would be the mother of two great nations: "And the LORD said to her, 'Two nations are in your womb, and two peoples from within you shall be divided; the one shall be stronger than the other, the older shall serve the younger'" (Genesis 25:23). And women continued to be central to the fulfillment of God's promise until the birth of Jesus.

Theotokos—Mary became the God-bearer (*theotokos*) by giving birth to Jesus Christ. Promise after promise, generation after generation, God kept the promise of salvation alive through women. In the fullness of time, the long-expected Savior was promised to Mary: "And the angel said to her, 'Do not be afraid, Mary, for you have found favor with God. And behold, you will conceive in your womb and bear a son, and you shall call His name Jesus. He will be great and will be called the Son of the Most High. And the Lord God will give to Him the throne of His father David, and He will reign over the house of Jacob forever, and of His kingdom there will be no end'" (Luke 1:30–33). The promise of a Savior traversed human history through women until the birth of Jesus. Mary conceived in her womb and became the only woman in human history to be used by God to interweave divinity and humanity in the person of Jesus.

These are just a few of the promises that God made specifically to women in the Bible. There is no question whatsoever: Scripture makes it clear that God relied heavily on women to deliver the promise of salvation. From Genesis to the Gospels and from Eve to Mary, the Bible stresses the special work of women in God's plan of salvation. The Bible esteems women as essential to God's plan of salvation.

However, it is not as if women sustained the salvation promise merely through childbearing. The Bible places women at the center of the most important moment of it all: the empty tomb of Jesus Christ. The first witnesses of the resurrection of Jesus were women. The Gospels celebrate women as the ones faithful to return to the tomb of Jesus:

> When the Sabbath was past, Mary Magdalene, Mary the mother of James, and Salome bought spices, so that they might go and anoint Him. And very early on the first day of the week, when the sun had risen, they went to the tomb. And they were saying to one another, "Who

will roll away the stone for us from the entrance of the tomb?" And looking up, they saw that the stone had been rolled back—it was very large. And entering the tomb, they saw a young man sitting on the right side, dressed in a white robe, and they were alarmed. And he said to them, "Do not be alarmed. You seek Jesus of Nazareth, who was crucified. He has risen; He is not here. See the place where they laid Him. But go, tell His disciples and Peter that He is going before you to Galilee. There you will see Him, just as He told you." (Mark 16:1–7)

The resurrection of Jesus is the focal point of Scripture. The Old Testament points to this moment, and the New Testament reflects on this moment. And faithful women are the first ones to the tomb. They are the first ones to hear the angelic proclamation that Jesus has risen from death to life.

A woman is also the first person to speak to the resurrected Jesus. Mary Magdalene encounters the resurrected Jesus at the tomb (John 20:11–18). Not knowing it was Jesus, Mary assumes that He is a gardener tending to the tombs. He speaks to her and she immediately realizes her mistake: "Jesus said to her, 'Mary.' She turned and said to Him in Aramaic, 'Rabboni!' (which means Teacher)" (John 20:16). The Bible reports with stunning boldness that women are the first to the empty tomb, first to hear the angelic proclamation, and first to encounter the resurrected Jesus.

This is irrefutable proof that the Bible does not dismiss, disrespect, or disregard women. It is impossible to deny that Scripture deems women so significant that they are central to the greatest Gospel moments in human history.

However, it is even more striking to place these first eyewitnesses in their historical context. During the time of Jesus, women were often relegated to the fringes of public life. Legal witnesses in the court of law were almost always men; women were often discredited or entirely barred from serving as an eyewitness in a legal testimony.

Nevertheless, the Bible relies on women as the first eyewitnesses of the empty tomb. Scripture relies on women to support the testimony of Jesus' resurrection. The Bible does not discredit women.

PROSTITUTES, CONCUBINES, AND RAPE

There is no denying the fact that the Bible has some gritty stuff in it. Among the grittiest parts of the Bible are the depictions of women being mistreated by men. There are numerous places in Scripture that reference prostitution (Genesis 38; Joshua 2; Judges 16:1), concubines (1 Kings 11:3; 2 Chronicles 11:21; Esther 2:14), and rape (Judges 19:22–26; 2 Samuel 13:10–14). As was previously stated in this chapter, these references to the mistreatment of women are descriptive and not prescriptive. The Bible encompasses many different genres throughout its many books; one of the most prominent genres in Scripture is historical narrative. The historical depictions in the Bible describe real events in all their gritty detail. The Bible does not offer a censored version of human history.

The instances of mistreatment of women in the Bible are descriptions of people acting against God's will. Do not confuse biblical descriptions of the mistreatment of women as prescribing these actions. This view of the Bible is entirely backward. Scripture makes it abundantly clear that it is God's will for women to be treated with the same dignity and worth as men. Scripture prescribes that women have intrinsic worth and value because God has fearfully and wonderfully created them. Women, as well as men, have been created in the image of God. Women, as well as men, have the breath of God filling their lungs. The precious blood of Jesus has ransomed both women and men.

WHAT ABOUT SUBMISSION?

To be certain, there are places in the Bible that prescribe differences between men and women. God gave certain curses to women

(Genesis 3:16) that He did not give to men. And God gave certain curses to men (Genesis 3:17–19) that He did not give to women. God accomplished certain plans through women that He did not accomplish through men (i.e., the Book of Ruth). And God accomplished certain plans through men that He did not accomplish through women (i.e., the Book of Jonah). This does not mean that there is inequality between women and men; but it does mean that God has different plans and purposes, calls and commissions for women and men.

Scripture prescribes clearly different responsibilities for women and men: "Wives, submit to your own husbands, as to the Lord. . . . Husbands, love your wives, as Christ loved the church and gave Himself up for her" (Ephesians 5:22, 25). There are many other places in the Bible that prescribe the different responsibilities of women and men (1 Corinthians 14:34; 1 Timothy 2:11–15; 1 Peter 3:5). The notion of men and women having different roles and responsibilities is deemed outlandish, outdated, and outmoded by modern society. Submission by either men or women is shunned by modern society as a sign of weakness and self-degradation.

Nevertheless, there is one problem with dismissing the sections of the Bible that prescribe different responsibilities: the persons of the Trinity—Father, Son, and Holy Spirit—have clearly different responsibilities. Furthermore, Jesus makes it clear that He willingly submits to the Father (Matthew 20:23; Mark 14:35–36; Luke 4:16–21). Jesus Christ, though He is entirely and completely God, submits to the Father. The different persons of the Trinity are fully and equally divine while still having unique responsibilities. Similarly, women and men are fully and equally created in the image of God. Both have intrinsic worth and value before God. These truths must be maintained while also maintaining the truth that God created men and women for unique purposes. These two truths are not mutually exclusive.

WHAT YOU NEED TO KNOW

Composed in a different time and culture, the Bible is clearly heavy on male figures and male authors. Scripture was composed long before modern movements for gender equality, women's suffrage, and feminism. Forcing modern standards on an ancient text is absurd. Why does the Bible not depict women voting in elections? For the exact same reason that the Bible does not depict people surfing the Internet, texting, and posting selfies.

Viewed within its historical and cultural context, the Bible is radically pro-women. God is depicted as making the first Gospel promise to a woman, keeping that promise alive through numerous other promises made to women, and finally bringing about the salvation of the world through Jesus Christ, born of a woman. As if that is not enough, women were the first eyewitnesses of the empty tomb and the resurrection of Jesus. When the rest of the ancient world was depreciating women, the Bible was delighting in their testimony of the Gospel of Jesus Christ.

There are numerous places in the Bible that describe the mistreatment of women. These historical descriptions are not prescribing these actions; instead, they function as an account of historical occurrences and as warnings to avoid repeating. There are certainly places in Scripture that prescribe different roles and responsibilities for wives and husbands; these differences in roles and responsibilities mirror the trinitarian relationship of the Father, Son, and Holy Spirit.

Encyclopedias

Roving salesmen used to go door to door enticing people to buy encyclopedias. This may seem like an arcane practice from a bygone age; after all, nobody is buying encyclopedia sets these days. Even the traveling vendors have since moved on to selling plastic food storage containers. And, depending on your age, you may even be wondering if an encyclopedia is some sort of wordplay on Wikipedia. It is not.

Encyclopedia sets were a really big deal at one time. People were not repulsed to hear the knock of the door-to-door encyclopedia salesman; people welcomed the opportunity to purchase a set of encyclopedias for their house. A multivolume set of encyclopedias allowed for any home to become a veritable library of knowledge. Until the invention of the Internet, people relied on a personal set of encyclopedias for a great deal of information.

The concept of an encyclopedia goes back nearly two thousand years. Pliny the Elder wrote one of the oldest known encyclopedias entitled *Naturalis Historia* in the first century (AD 77–79). He discussed topics ranging from astronomy and geography to art history and mining. This early encyclopedia led to thousands of other similar encyclopedias. While some encyclopedias focus on a specific topic or discipline, others are written to present a broad overview of many topics. For instance, the widely known Encyclopædia Britannica is a general-knowledge encyclopedia that has been issued in fifteen editions, beginning in 1768 to the final print edition in 2010. Like other encyclopedias, these volumes cover a wide range of topics with entries written by leading scholars and experts in a particular field.

Although encyclopedias are written by leading scholars and experts, they can still be all kinds of wrong. Take the Encyclopædia Britannica Eleventh Edition (1910–11) for example. This edition, like all other encyclopedias, was written by the top scholars of that day. The brightest and best minds of the early twentieth century were gathered together to create this tome of knowledge. Written just over a century ago, this so-called authority on knowledge is blatantly bigoted and biased. This relatively recent text is teeming with racism and chauvinism.

This encyclopedia makes numerous racist claims: The Ku Klux Klan is described as an asset to society helping to establish order in the American South and control African Americans. The entry entitled "Negro" described Africans as having a mental constitution similar to a child, uncultivated intellectual ability, and a "doglike fidelity," making them ideal servants. (This is no joke.) Elsewhere in the entry, leaders in the African American community are described as being invariably of mixed blood and deriving their leadership abilities from their white ancestry. This entry came from an "expert" on the topic.

This encyclopedia also makes numerous chauvinistic claims: Women are characterized as "invading" the professions of men. The entry explains that it is not possible for all women to become scholars, doctors, or lawyers; a career in one of these fields is especially difficult for women because they have to compete with men for the positions. The entry does, however, explain that women might be able to find a job as either a factory inspector or sanitary inspector. (Still not joking.) The eleventh edition of the Encyclopædia Britannica is curiously missing an entry for Marie Curie, even though she won the Nobel Prize for Physics in 1903 and the Nobel Prize for Chemistry in 1911. She is briefly mentioned in the volume . . . under her husband's entry.

It is important to note how this text—almost universally accepted as the authority on knowledge—is so woefully bigoted and biased. Although it is only a hundred years old, this encyclopedia is full of entries that misrepresent other races as inherently inferior. This text written by leading experts and scholars suggests that women are innately incompetent. Many of the scientific and medical entries are woefully inaccurate by modern standards. Only a century old and it is all kinds of wrong.

Compare this to the Bible: Thousands of years before this encyclopedia was written, the Bible was upholding the inherent dignity of other races. Thousands of years before some so-called expert claimed that women might not make the best lawyers, the Bible relied on women to be the key eyewitnesses to the resurrected Jesus. In just a hundred years, even the best encyclopedia became obsolete and out of touch with society. In more than two thousand years, God's Word has continued to promote the innate worth of all people regardless of skin color or gender.

STUDY QUESTIONS

1. The Bible has been wrongly used to promote racism. What are some other examples of a good thing being wrongly used?

2. Why is it so important to recognize the difference between description and prescription when reading the Bible?

3. Since Solomon enslaved certain people—and it's in the Bible!—does this mean that it is all right for other people to do it?

4. Scripture makes it clear that God's love is radically open to all people (Isaiah 56:1–8; Mark 16:15; Galatians 3:28). How are these verses even more powerful when placed in their historical context?

5. Why are religion and ethnicity often grouped together in Scripture?

6. What are some essential ways that God has relied on women in the Bible?

7. Does a difference in responsibilities automatically mean a difference in value?

9

OUTRAGEOUS AND OUTLANDISH

The Bible is outrageous and outlandish. And that is what makes it so great. Scripture is teeming with mind-bending miracles, wonderful works of God, and outlandish occurrences. Leaf through the Bible and you will find some incredible stuff: Moses parts a giant body of water, Jonah spends a few days in a fish, and Daniel has a sleepover with lions. Numerous dead people come back to life in the Bible: Tabitha, Eutychus, Lazarus, and a whole valley of dry bones. Countless hungry people have their bellies filled with food. Enemies of God come to know and love Him. Just about every page of the Bible contains something outrageous and outlandish.

And twice a year, the Church reads the most outlandish and outrageous portions of the entire Bible: the Scripture readings for Christmas and Easter. These are bold claims that stand out from every other bold claim made elsewhere in Scripture. The Christmas story is far from a cutesy tale about a lowly family having a baby in a manger; it is about the wonderfully powerful God of the universe uniting divinity with human flesh in the person of Jesus Christ. The Easter story makes no reference to bunnies or chocolates, pastel or pink; it is about God in human flesh offering His life on the cross, spending three days in the tomb vanquishing death and Satan, having His blood flow and human heat miraculously restored, and then rising victoriously to new life. These are bold claims. These are outlandish claims. These are outrageous claims. And these are true claims.

Many readers of the Bible attempt to do something curious with all these outrageous and outlandish claims: explain them away. Entire communities of believers read these texts and then begin spinning explanations for what really happened. Every dead person raised to new life was actually just sleeping. Every miraculous feeding was just a hidden stash of food. Jesus was not God; He was just a really good teacher. And He did not die on the cross but just swooned in pain and woke up three days later.

This is bogus.

The Bible makes outlandish and outrageous claims because they actually happened. Dead people actually came back to life. Food was actually multiplied. Blind eyes were really opened. Jesus actually is God in human flesh. He actually died. And He actually lives.

CLAIM:

MANY OF JESUS' MIRACLES GO AGAINST THE LAWS OF NATURE. YOU CANNOT POSSIBLY BELIEVE ALL THE MIRACLES ATTRIBUTED TO JESUS.

Any person making this claim is attempting to perform a miracle himself: forcing God into a box. Suggesting that God must conform to laws of nature is absurd. If God were small enough to be bound by the laws of nature, then He would certainly not be big enough to worship. The miracles of Jesus defy, deconstruct, and destroy the laws of nature.

There have been many attempts to explain away the miracles of Jesus. Outlandish does not begin to describe these explanations.

Scholars have tried to deconstruct every one of the miracles performed by Jesus:

- He used the wedding festivities as a distraction in order to switch jugs of water with jugs of wine (John 2:1–11).

- He stockpiled thousands of pieces of bread in a cave in order to feed the masses with what appeared to be only a few loaves (John 6:1–14).

- He used the power of persuasion in order to make people think that He had healed their demonic possession (Luke 8:26–39).

- He was able to call Lazarus from the tomb because he was not really dead (John 11:1–44).

This list could be three times longer. Skeptical scholars have an explanation for every one of the miracles performed by Jesus. They have deconstructed the details of every eye opened, unraveled the mystery behind every tongue loosed, and explained away every palsied limb made strong. These attempts at explaining away the miracles of Jesus require a miraculous amount of creativity, ingenuity, and wishful thinking. It is harder to disbelieve the miracles of Jesus than it is to believe.

The push to deconstruct the miracles of Jesus comes from an overestimation of the laws of nature. Science has established various laws of nature ranging from gravitation to thermodynamics. Scientists have determined the laws of nature to be universal and absolute. Apples on earth do not occasionally fall to the ground because of gravity; apples on earth always fall to the ground because of gravity. If it only occasionally happened that way, then it would not be a law of nature. Philosophers,

It is harder to disbelieve the miracles of Jesus than it is to believe.

theologians, historians, and scientists have applied these laws of nature to the miracles of Jesus and determined them completely incompatible: A child cannot be conceived without a father; thus Jesus could not be of divine birth. Human bodies are not buoyant enough to walk on water; thus Jesus could not have met the disciples in the middle of the lake. Dead people do not spontaneously come back to life; thus Jesus was not resurrected.

THE BIBLE > THE LAWS OF NATURE

These thinkers have wrongfully placed Jesus under the reign and rule of natural law. Making this claim is telling the God of the universe that He must conform to certain rules pertaining to matter and gravity. Arguing that the miracles of Jesus are concocted because they break the laws of nature forces God into a box. God did not give Moses any laws about gravitation at Mount Sinai. The laws of nature are human constructions; these supposed laws have come through careful observation and experimentation. God has clearly created the universe to work in a predictable way: Apples fall toward the earth. Hot air rises. Matter is neither created nor destroyed.

The problem is a man-made list of laws that God cannot break. God does not follow human rule books. He does not fit in test tubes. He defies human knowledge. Jesus turning water into wine is not breaking the laws of chemistry. He is simply God being God. Jesus walking on water is not an assault on buoyancy. This is simply what happens when God is present in creation. Jesus coming back to life after being dead for three days does not need to conform to the laws of nature. It is a miracle.

The miracles of Jesus were documented by a first-century Jewish historian named Josephus: "Now there was about this time Jesus, a wise man, if it be lawful to call him a man; for he was a doer of wonderful works, a teacher of such men as received the truth with pleasure" (*Antiquities of the Jews* 18.3.3). His wonderful works of turning water into wine, raising the dead, and healing the sick were noteworthy enough to be documented outside of the Bible. It is worth noting that skeptics have a rebuttal even to this extrabiblical corroboration of the miracles of Jesus; they claim that His followers secretly sneaked this line into the works of Josephus. This means not only that Jesus sneaked bread into a cave without anyone noticing, but also that His followers sneaked external evidence into Jewish writings to confirm the historicity of the miracles. (It sure is a lot of work disproving Jesus, huh?)

The miracles of Jesus were noteworthy enough to make it into extrabiblical works of history. And the miraculous works of Jesus were noteworthy enough to get Him killed. He performed them repeatedly and publicly. He raised the ire of religious leaders through His miracles. His miraculous deeds could not be deconstructed. Nobody could dismiss the work that Jesus was doing. The miracles performed by Jesus were so legitimate that the only recourse was to kill Him. And even that did not stop the miracles—He lives!

WHAT YOU NEED TO KNOW

God did not create the "laws" of nature per se. Humans devised these "laws" by observing God's creation and how it predictably functions. Forcing God to obey human laws of nature is laughable. The miracles of Jesus do not break the laws of nature; the miracles of Jesus show how creatures can never fully formulate their own Maker. Jesus performed miracles that are recorded in both the Bible and nonbiblical sources. His contemporaries could not easily deconstruct the miracles; it was easier to kill Jesus than explain away His miraculous works. Modern skeptics will have to do better than argue that Jesus had a stockpile of bread in a cave.

CLAIM:

IT IS OUTLANDISH TO THINK THAT SCRIPTURE
DEPICTS SALVATION AS BEING SIMPLY GRACE
ALONE THROUGH FAITH ALONE. THERE MUST
BE MORE TO IT.

Nope. No hoops to jump through. No time-share agreements to sign. God does not even make you prick your finger and sign your name in blood. God's plan of salvation is stunningly simple: Grace + Faith = Salvation. The Bible makes it overwhelmingly clear that God's plan of salvation is truly as simple as grace alone through faith alone:

- "After these things the word of the LORD came to Abram in a vision: 'Fear not, Abram, I am your shield; your reward shall be very great.' . . . And he believed the LORD, and He counted it to him as righteousness" (Genesis 15:1, 6).

- "But now the righteousness of God has been manifested apart from the law, although the Law and the Prophets bear witness to it—the righteousness of God through faith in Jesus Christ for all who believe. For there is no distinction: for all have sinned and fallen short of the glory of God, and are justified by His grace as a gift, through the redemption that is in Christ Jesus" (Romans 3:21–24).

- "For by grace you have been saved through faith. And this is not of your own doing; it is the gift of God, not a result of works, so that no one may boast" (Ephesians 2:8–9).

God's plan of salvation is stunningly simple. And it is powerfully profound. Probing the depths of grace and faith is anything but simple. Fully comprehending God's work of salvation is easily the most mind-bending, heart-wrenching, soul-stretching endeavor imaginable. Consider what God has done for you in Christ Jesus: He has poured out His grace for you in the life, death, and resurrection of

Jesus in an unmerited, undeserved, and completely unexpected deluge of divine love. Consider how God delivers this good gift to you individually: He fills you with the Holy Spirit so that you can have faith and thereby completely and utterly cling to Jesus as your Lord and Savior. None of this is your own doing; it is simply and totally the work of God freely given. You are saved by grace through faith in Jesus Christ. It is that simple.

The simplicity of salvation is constantly confused. There is constant temptation to add something more to God's plan of salvation: sacrifices, works, merits, good deeds, personal efforts, or human decisions. It is fairly easy to read through the Bible and confuse God's simple plan of salvation. Here are some ways in which people often get confused:

You are saved by grace through faith in Jesus Christ. It is that simple.

Sacrifices: The Old Testament is dripping with sacrifice. This practice is first mentioned in Genesis, further confirmed in Exodus, and then explained in great detail throughout Leviticus and Deuteronomy. Sacrifice does not disappear after the first five books of the Bible (known as the Pentateuch); the practice of sacrificing animals and food to God in an act of worship continues throughout the entire Old Testament. The practice of offering sacrifices to God continued even into the New Testament times. Mary and Joseph went to the temple to offer a sacrifice on behalf of their newborn child. Jesus went to the temple to celebrate feasts and offer a sacrifice in keeping with the Law. Peter and Paul were born Jewish and likely grew up offering sacrifices as well.

The sacrificial practices in Scripture were not meant to replace salvation by grace alone through faith alone. God used sacrifices as a way to deliver His grace in Christ Jesus. The blood of the Passover lamb was not efficacious apart from the grace of God shown in Christ Jesus; the sacrifices that God's people offered pointed them by faith to the once and for all sacrifice of Jesus on the cross. There is no confusion about it: salvation does not come through the blood of animals. Scripture never claims that God saved people through animal sacrifices in the Old Testament and now saves people by Jesus in the New Testament. The numerous sacrifices in the Bible all point to the once for all sacrifice of Jesus Christ on the cross. Salvation comes to all people—from Adam and Abraham to Zephaniah and Zechariah—through the grace of God shown in Christ Jesus. God did not change the plans of salvation at the birth of Jesus. Salvation has been, is now, and will always be by grace alone through faith alone.

Commandments: Others have tried to complicate salvation with human efforts to live a good life and follow the Commandments. It is easy to confuse the works that come from salvation with the works that lead to salvation. Good works do not lead to being saved; good works come from being saved. Following the Commandments does not lead to eternal life; eternal life leads to following the Commandments. Nevertheless, many readers of the Bible have claimed that following the Commandments, doing good deeds, trying your best, and deciding to commit your life to Jesus lead to salvation. This is a serious misunderstanding of Scripture. And it is a serious miscalculation of human ability.

Good works do not lead to being saved; good works come from being saved.

There are certainly places in the Bible that, when misunderstood, can lead people to believe that salvation relies on human effort. Take the conversation between Jesus and a rich young man for example: "And behold, a man came up to Him, saying 'Teacher, what good deed must I do to have eternal life?' And He said to him, 'Why do you ask Me about what is good? There is only one who is good. If you would enter life, keep the commandments'" (Matthew 19:16–17). This man asked Jesus how he could obtain eternal life and Jesus told him to keep the Commandments perfectly. Filled with arrogance—and maybe a hint of buffoonery—the rich young man responded by claiming to have kept all the Commandments without fail his entire life. Jesus then explained it to him another way: "Jesus said to him, 'If you would be perfect, go, sell what you possess and give to the poor, and you will have treasure in heaven; and come, follow Me'" (v. 21). At this point, the young man realized that he simply could not do this; he departed in sorrow because his sinful heart would not allow him to give up his many great possessions. The disciples were amazed by this interchange. With troubled eyes and mouths agape, the disciples asked a question: "Who then can be saved?" (v. 25). Jesus gave them the answer: "With man this is impossible, but with God all things are possible" (v. 26). On his own, this rich young man could not possibly keep the Commandments and merit his own salvation; the grace of God shown in Jesus and His perfect sacrifice, however, has done more than enough to merit eternal salvation.

Salvation is the work of God alone. Human effort, giving it your best, or doing good things are not a path to salvation. The Bible is not a handbook on how to be a good person. Scripture is not primarily about how to show love to God. It is exactly the opposite. The Bible is about how the grace of God covers your filthy soul with the precious blood of Jesus. God provides the grace and faith required for salvation. You receive it all with the empty hands of a beggar. And to God be the glory!

It is outlandish to think that salvation is as simple as grace alone through faith alone. It would seem that something as precious as eternal life should be more complex. Is it possible that assembling a coordinating outfit is more difficult than eternal salvation? Could it be that there are actually less steps to salvation than obtaining a valid passport? Can something so profound really be so simple? Yes. Yes. Yes. God does all the work of salvation. He provides the grace. He delivers the gift of faith. He makes all things new.

WHAT YOU NEED TO KNOW

God's plan of salvation is stunningly simple: Grace + Faith = Salvation. There are no steps to follow, rules to keep, or contracts to sign. God has poured out His abundant grace for you in the life, death, and resurrection of Jesus. He has delivered this good gift to you personally through the Holy Spirit. Salvation is not your own doing; it is simply and totally the work of God freely given. Although there are numerous references to offering sacrifices and doing good deeds in the Bible, these are not to be confused with a path to salvation. Both sacrifices and commandments find their purpose and meaning in the grace of God shown in Christ Jesus. The biblical practice of offering sacrifices to God was never meant to replace the blood of Jesus; the blood of animal sacrifices pointed God's people to the greater sacrifice of Jesus on the cross. Following God's commandments is not a path to salvation. Rather, our failure to follow God's commandments drives a nail into our prideful hearts. Good works do not lead to eternal life; good works come as a result of eternal life. Scripture makes a clear and consistent claim: God's plan of salvation is stunningly simple. Eternal life is found in Christ Jesus alone by grace alone through faith alone.

CLAIM:

THE BIBLE IS JUST ONE OF MANY HOLY BOOKS. IT IS OUTRAGEOUS TO THINK THAT IT IS RIGHT AND ALL OTHERS ARE WRONG.

It certainly is outrageous to claim that the Bible is right and all other holy books are wrong. Yet it is even more outrageous to claim that every holy book ever written is right. Claiming that every holy book ever written is equally true is an outrage to logical thinking. The many different holy books read by people today—the Book of Mormon, the Qur'an, the Bhagavad Gita, *Science and Health*, the Bible, and many others—make claims that are fundamentally incompatible with one another. It requires a great deal of mental gymnastics, creative interpretation, and wishful thinking in order to synthesize these holy books. There is an academic discipline known as comparative religion that does just this. Scholars in this discipline attempt to demonstrate how holy books address the same issues and make the same claims.

One of the most famous axioms to come out of the field of comparative religions is "All religions are essentially about being a good person." This would mean that all holy books are essentially handbooks for being good. According to this logic, the Bible and the Book of Mormon and the Bhagavad Gita are all similar to one another because they guide people in being good. The problem with this axiom is that it blurs, botches, and bungles the central message of Scripture. The Bible is not about simply being a good person. God's Word is not a handbook for holiness, a path to prosperity, or a guide to the good life.

The Bible is about what God has done for you in human history through the life, death, and resurrection of Jesus. It is more than wise words and encouraging expressions. It is not a list of ways to please God or obtain good health. The gravitational core of the Bible is the Good News of Jesus Christ: God's promise of a Savior, the formation of a chosen people, the mysterious arrival of God in human flesh, Jesus' authoritative teaching and sacrificial death, the glorious empty tomb of Jesus, and the eternal life that God has procured for you.

This all has very little to do with you being a good person. If there is any aspect of the Bible that is about being a good person, then it is about how God has painstakingly made you an entirely new and good person through the death and resurrection of Jesus Christ. The Bible is about what God has done for you rather than what you need to do for God. The Bible is unlike any other holy book on account of Jesus. He has performed the work necessary for the forgiveness of your sins. No other holy book contains anything close to divine grace disrupting sin, the Creator taking on flesh and blood, and engaging real historical kingdoms with the heavenly kingdom of God. Other holy books simply do not make these claims. Here are some of the substantial differences that set the Bible apart from any other holy book:

Guidance: Other holy books claim to offer guidance. The Qur'an, the holy book of Muslims, offers guidance for how to live a just and moral life according to the will of Allah. *Science and Health*, the holy book of Christian Science, is likened to a textbook since it depicts healing methods that are foundational to the religion. The Book of Mormon, the primary holy book of the Church of Jesus Christ of Latter-day Saints, claims to be guidance revealed to prophets about how to overcome sin and obtain salvation. The Bhagavad Gita, one of the many holy books of Hinduism, advises readers to establish dharma by living the right way. Pick almost any holy book and you will find guidance for how to live a moral, holy, and good life.

The heart of Scripture is Gospel, not guidance. Pick up the Bible and you will find that it is not fixated on offering advice. Certainly the Bible offers guidance for how to live as one redeemed by God. Nevertheless, the Bible is primarily good news about what God has done for you in Christ Jesus. Holy Scripture is about the promise of God made in the beginning, sustained through generations, delivered in a lowly manger, and confirmed victorious with the empty tomb of Jesus Christ. This is not guidance; this is good news proclaimed to sinners.

Demands: Other holy books are full of demands. Salvation is contingent on meeting a long list of demands. Pilgrimages, offerings, good works, and pure hearts are just the beginning of the countless demands set forth by other holy books. Being a good person depends on your ability to meet these demands. Earning divine favor is subject to how well you can uphold these obligations. Other holy books offer a path to follow, a plan to uphold, or a promise to keep: if you do these things, then you will receive salvation.

The Bible is not a collection of commands, a digest of demands, or a list of outlandish obligations. The Bible proclaims that God has fulfilled the demands on your behalf in Christ Jesus. Scripture speaks comfort to people overwhelmed with far too many demands; God has followed the path of salvation without fail, upheld the plan of salvation perfectly, and kept absolutely every promise. The Bible is not just another holy book with a list of demands that you must keep; the Bible proclaims how the love of God has already met the demands for you in Christ Jesus.

Holy Words: Other holy books claim to be filled with holy words. Gnostic writings from the second century claim to be holy words that could impart secret knowledge. In the seventh century, the Qur'an came to Muhammad through the angel Gabriel without any human interaction; the prophet served as a secretary and captured the divine word verbatim. In the nineteenth century, the Book of Mormon came to Joseph Smith when the angel Moroni directed him to golden plates engraved with holy words. These holy books all claim to be holy words that are completely divine, without human interaction, and free from error. Like water going through a pipe, these holy words went from divine source to human text. These books claim to have timeless and eternal words that more or less descended from heaven.

To be absolutely certain—the Bible does claim to be holy words. It is called the Holy Bible for a reason. The Bible is the Word of God. Thus it is a holy book with holy words. Nevertheless, the Bible is far more than just holy words that descended from heaven. The words and events of the Bible are actual occurrences in human history. The historical life, death, and resurrection of Jesus makes the Bible unlike any other religious text. The living person of Jesus separates the Bible from every other holy book in history and around the globe.

The holy words and claims of the Bible can be corroborated by actual historical evidence. Archaeologists have unearthed proof of enslaved Hebrews in Egypt, King David's reign, and the existence of Pontius Pilate. These discoveries—and the thousands of others like them—are proof that the Bible is more than just holy words. Scripture is both God's Word and God's work in human history. The Bible is the timeless and eternal Word of God spoken into a specific time in human history. And it is the tremendously timely work of God in human history. The Bible is both God's holy words and God's holy work. No other holy book can claim the level of historical corroboration supporting the Bible.

WHAT YOU NEED TO KNOW

It is outrageous by modern standards to claim that the Bible is right and every other holy book is wrong. It grinds postmodern sensibilities to hear anyone claim that one book is true and others are false. It sounds like nails on a chalkboard for modern ears to hear anyone claim that the Bible is the Word of God and the only true holy book.

The Bible is unlike any other holy book. God's Word does not offer guidance for how to be a good person, a list of demands for earning salvation, or empty words detached from history. Scripture proclaims the promise of God made in the beginning, sustained through generations, delivered in a lowly manger, and confirmed victorious with the empty tomb of Jesus Christ. This is good news for all creation. This is good news for sinners. And this is good news for you.

The Book of Mormon

The Bible did not fall out of the sky leather-bound and ready to read. The Holy Spirit inspired many different human authors over many generations to compose and compile the Word of God. There is not one single human author of the Bible. There is not one single editor of the Bible. There is not one single moment in which the Bible came into existence. The Bible did not fall out of the sky.

The Book of Mormon did. At least, that is essentially what some people claim.

Its proper title is *The Book of Mormon: Another Testament of Jesus Christ.* This text proposes to be a record of God's dealings with the ancient inhabitants of the Americas. The book contains the writings of many ancient prophets gathered together by the prophet historian Mormon. The revelations in the Book of Mormon depict events that happened between 2200 BC and AD 421.

Much like the Bible, the Book of Mormon consists of many smaller books named after an author or narrator: 1 Nephi, 2 Nephi, Enos, Jarom, Mormon, Moroni, and others. The crowning event of the book is the personal ministry of Jesus Christ among the Nephites in the ancient Americas. During this interaction, Jesus supposedly gave further teaching on the plan of salvation and eternal life. The Book of Mormon alleges to have prophetic teachings that are not contained in the Bible.

If you think that the contents of the Book of Mormon are outrageous and outlandish, the discovery of it is even more outrageous and outlandish. The Book of Mormon was delivered to Joseph Smith (1805–44) by an angel of God named Moroni. As the story goes, when Smith was only seventeen years old, the angel Moroni appeared to him and advised him that there was a collection of golden plates buried in western New York. This angelic vision happened on the evening of September 21, 1823. The next day, Smith met with Moroni on the hill where the golden plates were buried and was told that he had to wait four years to bring them forth from the ground. Exactly four years later, Smith unearthed them and began translating the contents of the golden plates into English.

The golden plates were etched with hieroglyphics. Smith claimed that he received special eyeglasses that allowed him to translate the plates into English. There are other claims that Smith used a top hat and seer stones to translate the text. Smith relied on a scribe to write down the text in English as he translated it from the plates. Much of this transcribing was done with Smith on one side of a curtain and the transcriber on the other side unable to see what Smith was doing. There were, however, eleven witnesses who claimed to have seen the golden plates. Almost immediately after Smith published the books, critics began accusing him of entirely fabricating and forging the book from other works. The Book of Mormon bares striking similarities to the King James Bible and two other books that were popular in Smith's day, *The Wonders of Nature* (1826) and *View of the Hebrews* (1823). There are even numerous direct quotes from the King James Bible in the Book of Mormon; for instance, the Second Book of Nephi contains eighteen quoted chapters from the Book of Isaiah.

Manuscript evidence for the Book of Mormon is lacking. Smith created three manuscripts from the golden plates. The first manuscript—known as the original manuscript—was placed in the walls of a house (the Nauvoo House) that Joseph Smith had built. After forty years of being sealed up in the walls, the manuscript had deteriorated considerably and was nearly ruined. Only 28 percent of the original manuscript survives today and is kept by the Church of Jesus Christ of Latter-day Saints. There is a second copy of the text that was used for printing. This printer's copy is still in existence today and is the oldest intact copy of the Book of Mormon.

There are many questions surrounding the Book of Mormon—questionable sources, questionable content, and questionable manuscript evidence. And these are only the beginning of the questions surrounding this text. Compared to the Bible, the Book of Mormon comes up severely wanting in credibility. The Bible did not come into existence through the work of one person behind a curtain. The Bible did not fall out of the sky etched on golden plates that required special glasses for deciphering. Although the account of how the Bible came into existence may be less fantastical, it is far more credible. Scripture involved many human authors writing by the inspiration of the Holy Spirit over many generations. There are a few thousand manuscript witnesses for the Bible. No angels delivering holy books on a hill. No lost tribes of Israel in America. No reformed hieroglyphics. The Bible is the eternally trustworthy Word of God. Nothing more. Nothing less.

STUDY QUESTIONS

CHAPTER 9

1. What do you think is the most outlandish claim in all of Scripture?

2. How is it harder to disbelieve the miracles of Jesus than it is to believe them?

3. Why do people often want to make salvation more complicated than it is?

4. If salvation in the Old Testament was not based on sacrifices, then why would God command them?

5. "All religions are essentially about being a good person." How does this statement misrepresent the message of Scripture?

6. If the Bible is about the life, death, and resurrection of Jesus, then does that mean it does not offer any guidance at all?

7. Why is it so outrageous by modern standards to claim that the Bible is right and every other holy book is wrong?

CONCLUSION

Y ou have now examined numerous claims against the Bible. You have considered many reasons as to why these claims cannot be substantiated. You have explored other reputable texts and seen the ways that they are lacking when compared to the Bible. You may have even picked up some ten-dollar words along the way. All of this was to help you answer the question "Why should I trust the Bible?"

Now you have it all figured out. You will never encounter a claim against the Bible that you cannot refute. You will never again be speechless, scratching your head, and looking down at your feet when someone raises a question about the trustworthiness of Scripture. You now have all the answers you could possibly need to defend the Bible. . . .

Who am I kidding?!? This is simply not true. And if you think this is true, prepare to be disappointed. You will inevitably encounter questions about the Bible that were not addressed in this humble book. You will meet someone with difficult questions for which there are no easy answers. You probably had your own issues with the Bible that were not resolved in the previous pages. Even if you did not, you will certainly have more quandaries, queries, and questions as you walk with Jesus in the days ahead.

Keep going. Press on. Lean in. Pray that the Holy Spirit would engage your whole heart and your whole mind in answering these questions. Read more books about the Bible, study Scripture with others, and ask difficult questions. And above all, keep following Jesus. He is at the center of Scripture. He is the Word made flesh. Jesus is the real and living person around whom the Bible coheres. And He is the one and only source of eternal life:

> After this many of His disciples turned back and no longer walked with Him. So Jesus said to the Twelve, "Do you want to go away as well?" Simon Peter answered Him, "Lord, to whom shall we go? You have the words of eternal life, and we have believed, and have come to know, that you are the Holy One of God." (John 6:66–69)

LEADER GUIDE

CHAPTER 1 STUDY QUESTIONS

1. Why is it important that Jesus is the foundation for trust in the Bible?

The Christian faith is centered on Jesus Christ. Everything else—local congregations, worship services, ministry activities, and books like this one—exist only to support us as we follow Jesus. Our faith is founded on Christ alone, and He is our salvation. Just as Jesus is the foundation for our faith, He is also the foundation for our trust in the Bible. Unlike anything else, trust in Jesus does not fail.

2. Who were some eyewitnesses of the resurrection of Jesus?

Many people had ocular proof of Jesus' resurrection. A few of these individuals include the women at the tomb (Matthew 28:1–10), Mary Magdalene (John 20:11–18), Peter (Luke 24:34), Cleopas and another disciple (Luke 24:13–35), the ten disciples excluding Judas and Thomas (John 20:19–23), Thomas (John 20:24–29), five hundred people (1 Corinthians 15:6), and numerous others.

3. Eyewitness testimony was trusted in the ancient world. Do people still rely on the account of an eyewitness today?

There are countless ways in which people still rely on eyewitness accounts. The most obvious is in the modern judicial system, which relies on eyewitness testimony to reach a verdict. However, there are many other ways that ocular proof is trusted. Scientists view and record test results with their eyes and thereby establish data. Travelers witness places with their eyes and then report their experience to others. Friends see a movie and then offer a trust-worthy account of what happened. Much of our knowledge is established by eyewitness testimony.

4. **Are there other instances in Scripture besides the resurrection where eyewitness accounts are relied upon?**

Eyewitness accounts are relied upon throughout Scripture. An example of this is found in Deuteronomy 17:6: "On the evidence of two witnesses or of three witnesses the one who is to die shall be put to death; a person shall not be put to death on the evidence of one witness." It is important to note a couple things from this example. First, evidence must be corroborated from multiple eyewitnesses; this is an attempt to protect against false witnesses. Second, eyewitness testimony has the authority to determine a substantial punishment. Other examples of eyewitness testimony in the Bible include Joshua 24:19–28; Ruth 4; Jeremiah 32:1–15.

5. **There are numerous creeds in the Bible. Some examples include Deuteronomy 6:4 and Romans 10:9. Why were creedal confessions so important in the ancient world? Why are creedal confessions still important today?**

Knowing core creedal statements was important in the ancient world because written texts were not always readily available. Traveling with scrolls and texts was impractical and difficult. Many individuals were unable to access biblical texts. Therefore, it was vital for people to know certain core confessions of the faith so they could recite them from memory. The same is true for people today. Even though it is far easier for modern followers of Jesus to access biblical text, it is still vitally important to have confessions of faith memorized and ready to recall in the moment.

6. **Why is the resurrection of Jesus included in all of the Gospels while other events are included in only a few of the Gospels?**

When the Bible mentions something once, then it is important. When the Bible mentions something multiple times, then it is *extremely* important. For example, God guides His people saying, "You shall love the LORD your God with all your heart and with all your soul and with all your might" (Deuteronomy 6:5). This command is echoed in many other places throughout Scripture (Matthew 22:37; Mark 12:30; Luke 10:27). It is obvious that this is an important command because of its reoccurrence throughout the Bible. The same is true for the resurrection of Jesus; this event is central to all of Scripture and is therefore prominent in numerous places.

7. **Why is external evidence important for establishing trust in the Bible?**

There are many other holy books claiming to be divine based on internal evidence. In order to set the Bible apart from these so-called holy books, it is important to recognize how the Bible can be externally validated. The Bible does not make hollow claims of holiness; the Bible makes hefty claims that can be historically confirmed.

CHAPTER 2 STUDY QUESTIONS

1. **What other creation accounts are you aware of? How do they depict the creation of the world?**

Answers may vary, as there are countless other creation accounts from many different places and cultures. Native American tribes have a panoply of different creation accounts that involve bears and birds, corn and mud. Creation accounts from Asia often depict the world as coming from a primordial egg. Another account coming out of India depicts a god—Brahma—creating the world, then becoming man and woman, and then becoming many different animals. The diversity and creativity in ancient creation accounts is staggering.

2. **What comes to mind when you hear the word *myth*?**

"Myth" has many different connotations. Sometimes "myth" can refer to a completely fanciful tale along the lines of Paul Bunyan and Babe the Blue Ox. Other times, "myth" can refer to an ancient story that a previous society believed to be true but modern society has rejected as false. And, yet other times, "myth" describes a story told to reinforce a certain moral virtue. It is important to note that "myth" means more than simply false or fiction.

3. **The creation account in the Bible is not a fanciful myth. How does Scripture make it clear that it is not merely mythology?**

There are numerous places in Scripture that portray Adam as a historically real individual (1 Chronicles 1:1–27; Hosea 6:7; Luke 3:38; 1 Timothy 2:13). These instances make it impossible to read Genesis as a placeless, timeless, imagined myth. The entirety of

Scripture handles the creation account in Genesis as more than a myth. There is nothing to suggest that this should be read as a fanciful tale.

4. God's Word is powerful. What are some ways that you have experienced the power of God's Word in your own life?

The Word of God is far more powerful than mere human words. It creates and sustains, kills and makes alive, judges and sets free. Hearing the Law enables you to experience a powerful encounter with God's will and a call to repentance from sin. Hearing the Gospel creates a powerful encounter with the mercy of God shown in Christ Jesus. You do not read God's Word as much as God's Word "reads" you: Scripture "reads" you by exposing your sins, unearthing your need for a Savior, and rewriting your future with eternal hope.

5. Read Genesis 6:11–22. Who is the central figure in this text?

Noah would appear to be the central figure of this text. However, a closer look at the verses reveals that it is actually God. It is important to notice that, grammatically speaking, God is the subject and Noah is the object. Although Noah is the one being addressed, God is the one who sees a creation filled with violence, resolves to cleanse the earth of corruption, and devises a plan to save Noah and his family. God establishes the covenant with Noah.

6. Many other flood narratives depict a human as the central figure of the text. Why might these false narratives put humans at the center?

Sin causes us to be curved away from God and turned in on ourselves. It is no surprise that many other false flood narratives from antiquity try to rewrite the truth by putting the focus on humans. Apart from salvation in Jesus, the human heart is set on sin and selfishness.

7. Why is it important to know of the existence of other ancient flood narratives?

Ignorance may be blissful, but it is not beneficial. It is vital for readers of the Bible to know that other ancient flood narratives exist so that these false accounts can be properly understood. Suppose you are having a conversation with someone about the Bible and she brings up these conflicting flood narratives. Your authority and credibility increases if you are aware of these accounts and have a reasonable defense against them.

CHAPTER 3 STUDY QUESTIONS

1. **Why might people intentionally try to find errors in the Bible?**

Jesus made it clear to His disciples that they should expect people to hate them on account of Him (John 15:18–19). Therefore, it is no surprise that people would try to poke holes in the Bible since it extols the name of Jesus. Satan is always opposed to the proclamation of the Gospel.

2. **Why is it important to learn about the manuscript witnesses that support the Bible?**

First, these manuscripts are the basis for the modern versions of the Bible. Just as a chef needs to know about the individual ingredients used in a recipe, it is important for a Bible reader to know about the individual components used to create the biblical text. Second, the vast array of manuscript witnesses supporting the Bible far exceeds that of any other ancient text. These manuscripts are proof that the Bible is trustworthy.

3. **There are significantly more New Testament manuscript witnesses than Old Testament manuscript witnesses. What caused this disproportionate number of manuscripts?**

This has to do with the culture and period of history in which these texts were written. The Greco-Roman world enjoyed widespread literacy and writing material. It is important to note that the smaller number of Old Testament manuscript witnesses is similar to other ancient texts from the same time period.

4. **Is there any way that the existence of textual variants actually adds to the trustworthiness of the Bible?**

The existence of textual variants can actually be used as proof that the Bible is trustworthy. These variant readings demonstrate the complete and total transparency of the Bible. Nobody is hiding anything. The complete inventory of manuscripts—even those that complicate the text—are available for everyone to see. There would be reason for concern if an ancient text copied over many generations had no variations whatsoever. However, it is important to note that the textual variants are extremely minor and do not compromise the message of the Bible.

5. **The Bible was written fully by God but also fully by humans. What other aspects of the Christian faith share this same paradoxical tension?**

There are a number of difficult tensions within the Christian faith. Jesus is not half man, half God; Jesus is fully divine and fully human. Holy Communion is not half bread and wine, half Christ's body and blood; it is fully Christ's body and blood and fully bread and wine. Faith in Jesus does not make you half saved, half sinful; you are fully redeemed by Jesus yet still fully a sinner in need of a Savior. The tension of the Bible being fully the divine Word of God composed through human authors is similar to many other core Christian teachings.

6. **The Holy Spirit connects people to Jesus. Why is it important to recognize the work of the Holy Spirit in writing the Bible?**

Without the inspiration of the Holy Spirit, the Bible would be a human text devoid of any real power. It is important to recognize the work of the Holy Spirit in composing the Bible because this distinguishes it from any other text. It is the Word of God because

God's Spirit breathed life into every single word. Furthermore, the work of the Holy Spirit is to be a witness to Jesus. Since the Holy Spirit inspired the Bible, it follows that the Bible is primarily a witness to Jesus.

7. **What part of the composition process did the Holy Spirit inspire?**

The Holy Spirit was active throughout the composition process. There is no reason to believe that the Holy Spirit was active only during certain parts of the composition process. God actively guided the biblical authors in the planning, drafting, composing, and editing of the Scriptures. And the Holy Spirit continued to guide the formation of the Bible through the canonization process.

CHAPTER 4 STUDY QUESTIONS

1. What are some arguments people have made in order to discredit the history contained in the Bible?

Skeptics have used every angle you could imagine in their attempt to discredit the history contained in the Bible. Some have claimed that the Bible concocts history as a sort of religious propaganda. Others have suggested that the Bible is a chauvinistic, male-dominated version of history. Some scholars have depicted Scripture as being simply ancient Israelite nationalism. Yet others have argued that the Bible is concerned only with spiritual matters and therefore does not bother with accurately depicting historical events.

2. How does the Bible prove these arguments incorrect?

The content and context of the Bible demonstrates that its history is reliable. The content of the Bible reveals that it is not a censored or cleaned-up rendition of history; rather, the Bible contains the good and the bad, the victories and the defeats. Furthermore, the historical context that gave rise to Scripture was seldom a place of power. Many of the books of the Bible were composed from places of subjugation rather than places of domination. History written by the victors should be read with suspicion; the Bible was more often written by the impoverished and imprisoned.

3. Are there other ways the history in the Bible is proved accurate?

Archaeology is an external source that proves the history of the Bible is trustworthy. There have been numerous instances in which archaeologists have made discoveries verifying the history of the Bible. To be certain, trust in the Bible does not center on these archaeological discoveries. Nevertheless, they do provide further confirmation of the historicity of Scripture.

4. How did differences in audience influence the contents of the Gospels?

The Gospels were not written to the exact same communities. Each Gospel has a unique audience with different assumptions, values, and concerns. The differences in audience influence what content is included or excluded, what words are used or explained, what geographic areas receive special focus, and even what calendars are accepted for chronology. Many of the differences in the Gospels are a result of different authors writing to different audiences.

5. Why is it important to know how to refute the supposed inaccuracies in the Gospels?

The Good News of Jesus Christ is about God engaging human history. In order for something to be considered "news," it must happen within time and space. The historical accuracy of the Gospels is important because the Gospels depict real happenings in history. If the Gospel is full of historical inaccuracies, then the Good News of Jesus is seriously compromised. It is therefore important to know how to refute these supposed historical inaccuracies and defend the Gospel.

6. Should Christians ask difficult questions about the historical timeline of the Gospels?

Yes. Yes. Yes. It is the responsibility of any serious Bible reader to ask difficult questions. There is no reason your brain should be put on autopilot while reading Scripture. Engage the Bible with your whole heart and mind. This is what the church in Berea did

(Acts 17) when Paul came to proclaim the Gospel to them. Study the Scriptures, ask hard questions, and seek faithful answers.

7. How are the historical accounts in Shakespeare's plays similar to historical accounts in the Gospels?

Shakespeare depicted actual historical events in his dramas. Nevertheless, these dramas were not intended to depict the whole breadth of English history; Shakespeare was using snippets of history as the basis for his dramas. In the same way, the Gospels include actual historical events that took place in the Roman Empire during the first century. However, these historical events are included and ordered around the life and ministry of Jesus. The point of the Gospels is not to tell the complete history of the ancient world; the point of the Gospels is to tell the world of how God has entered into human history to bring salvation in Jesus Christ (John 20:30–31).

CHAPTER 5 STUDY QUESTIONS

1. **What is the appeal to claiming there are "secret books" that were excluded from the Bible?**

Scandals and secrecy, censorship and conspiracy provide for an interesting story. Television programs and popular books are more likely to draw an audience if they depict the formation of the biblical canon as a massive scandal. The appeal is in selling commercials and copies of books—not in telling the truth. Satan revels in misinformation and obscuring the truth (see John 8:44).

2. **Why is the account of Serapion of Antioch helpful in seeing how the Early Church sorted through which texts to use?**

The example of Serapion of Antioch demonstrates how open and transparent the Early Church was in determining which texts to use for worship. There was no secrecy behind what Serapion did; he shared with his congregation the reasons why the Gospel of Peter should not be used. He was concerned that the author of the text was not Peter and that no other Christian congregation had handed the text down for use in worship. By doing this, Serapion was following the instructions Paul gave to Timothy in 1 Timothy 6.

3. **The Early Church used different categories for classifying texts when deciding whether they should be included in the biblical canon or not. What were these different categories?**

The texts were classified as either *homologoumena, antilegomena,* or heretical. The *homologoumena* texts were those the Early Church unanimously agreed to include in the canon. If there were some reservations about a text as to its author or origin, then it was considered *antilegomena*. And texts that were rejected outright as spurious were considered heretical.

4. **The canon was not determined by putting books on an altar and waiting for some to fall down. Could God have directed the formation of the canon even if it did not happen miraculously?**

God works through ordinary means. Something does not have to be miraculous in order for it to be the work of God. Just as Jesus used dirt and spit to heal a man's eyes (John 9), the Holy Spirit worked through individuals and local congregations in order to determine which books were to be included in the Bible. The formation of the canon was supernatural (directed by God), yet accomplished through extremely ordinary means (average people).

5. **What are some ancient nonbiblical texts that offer a depiction of Jesus?**

There are numerous ancient texts depicting Jesus that were not included in the Bible. The Early Church produced many different texts during the formation of the biblical canon. There is strong evidence to suggest that Paul wrote many other epistles not included in the Bible. Similarly, there were Early Church writings (for example, the *Didache*) that were excluded from the Bible. Unlike these other texts, there were also Gnostic texts that offered a grossly distorted depiction of Jesus for use by an entirely different religion referred to as Gnosticism.

6. **Who were some influential Early Church writers defending the faith from false teaching?**

A number of Early Church leaders took up the fight to defend the Bible. Origen openly called for the Church to stand up against misinformation parading around as truth. Another influential Early Church leader was Eusebius. He wrote *Church History*, which allowed all to see how the formation of the Bible occurred. These writers, and many others in the Early Church, defended the faith through open and transparent dialogue.

7. How is Gnosticism fundamentally different from Christianity?

The Gnostic religion centers on a rejection of the material world and a reliance on hidden wisdom that leads to salvation. This is a radical departure from the Christian belief that the created world is good because God made it. Furthermore, the Gospel is not secret or hidden knowledge; it is intended to be freely and openly proclaimed to all people. Gnosticism shares little in common with Christianity.

CHAPTER 6 STUDY QUESTIONS

1. What texts do people rightfully regard as old and obsolete?

As texts age, they do have a tendency to become obsolete. Since writing is contextual, it makes sense that changing contexts can render a text outdated. Owner's manuals for antiquated appliances (rotary phones, typewriters, transistor radios) are no longer regarded as helpful texts. Political writings full of rejected ideologies (Adolf Hitler's *Mein Kampf*) are rightfully rejected as obsolete. People now read these texts for their historical value rather than their contemporary relevancy.

2. What are some examples of modern thinkers being misguided in their thinking?

Modern thinkers can be just as wrong as ancient thinkers. Just a few generations ago, reputable doctors suggested smoking cigarettes as a digestive aid. A few generations before that, doctors suggested drawing blood to help fight illnesses. The Holocaust is a clear example of modern thinkers being completely misguided in their thinking. These examples make it clear that modern thinkers do not always know better than ancient thinkers.

3. Read Romans 1:19–20. Are these words of Paul an example of general revelation or special revelation?

These verses describe what is known as general revelation. God provides a general revelation of Himself in the natural world. The order of the universe reveals that an orderly Creator formed it. The beauty of God's creation makes it clear that God delights in beauty. When people use God's creation to produce works of art and literature, these creations can provide a general revelation of God.

4. **Read Matthew 28:18–20. Are these words of Jesus an example of general revelation or special revelation?**

It would be impossible to know these words of Jesus apart from them being revealed directly by God. Nobody could learn of the Great Commission by reading a work of literature or viewing a beautiful sunset. These words of Jesus are an example of special revelation that will never become old or obsolete.

5. **What is required in order for something to be considered "news"?**

News happens within a specific time and place. For instance, the stock market crashed on October 24, 1929, in New York City. News also occurs within a preexisting context, and it reshapes the future context. For instance, the crash of the stock market occurred within the broader context of global uncertainty following World War I, and it resulted in sustained economic turmoil.

6. **Why is the good news of Jesus Christ rightly considered "news"?**

Like any news, the birth of Jesus occurred at a certain time and in a certain place. He was born into the political context of the Roman Empire. More broadly speaking, Jesus was born into the context of a creation marred by sin. His life, death, and resurrection forever reshaped the context of this world by undoing the power of sin and ushering in eternal life. The Gospel is not mere opinion or advice.

7. **The Bible speaks loud and clear to contemporary culture. How is the Bible speaking loud and clear in your life lately?**

The answer to this question is obviously rather personal. However, it is powerful to recognize the ways in which God's Word speaks afresh to us every new day. The reason for this is not that God's Word changes. Rather, the Holy Spirit engages us with God's Word and speaks in the midst of our present troubles and fears, hopes and needs. Reading the Bible is never a static experience.

CHAPTER 7 STUDY QUESTIONS

1. **How much of a difference is there between translations of the Bible and the original text?**

The difference between the original text of the Bible and modern translations of it is minimal. The differences are so slight that only trained experts could recognize these discrepancies. Furthermore, the differences are never intended to obscure the text but instead to clarify it. An example of this is when a translation takes a biblical idiom and rephrases it to make sense in the receptor language.

2. **Have you ever seen a live production of a play you first saw on video? What were the differences between the productions?**

Answers to this question will vary, but the differences were most likely periphery and nonessential to the plot line. Perhaps the producer concluded the live production with a lecture on the play or the video had a commentary by the actors and actresses. The differences likely had to do with viewing angle, lighting, and sound.

3. **How is reading a translation of the Bible similar to viewing a video recording of a play?**

Translations of the Bible are in many ways similar to video reproductions of a play. In both instances, the overall message and story is the same across the different versions. It is not as if the translation of the Bible or the video version of a play somehow tell an entirely different story. There certainly are differences between the versions; however, these differences do not hinder the faithful delivery of the work.

4. **What are the three different methodologies that guide Bible translators in their work?**

The three methodologies are dynamic equivalence, formal equivalence, and paraphrasing. One aims to translate the Bible thought-for-thought (dynamic equivalence), another aims at translating the Bible word-for-word (formal equivalence), and the last aims at the most accessible and readable version possible (paraphrasing). The methodology employed by a Bible translator has a profound impact on the final translation of the text.

5. **The United States Constitution is an important document. What are some different interpretations of this text?**

The United States Constitution has been subjected to a multiplicity of interpretations. For instance, *originalism* is a principle of interpretation that views the Constitution's meaning as fixed as of the time it was written. Determining the best interpretation of the constitution is known as judicial interpretation.

6. **Interpretation is a communal practice. How have you seen this statement in action?**

Perhaps right now. You may be discussing these questions in a small group or a Bible study setting. That means that you are interpreting this book within a community of other people. The same happens when you gather for Bible study, discuss the sermon with someone else, or talk about a novel with your neighbor. Interpretation of the Bible always takes place within an interpretive community.

7. Why is it a "good fight" to defend the Bible from wildly divergent interpretations?

Throughout Scripture, God's people are encouraged to walk along straight paths (Proverbs 4:20–27). This means that we are to avoid diverging into crooked paths of falsehood. It is never a good idea to argue simply for the sake of arguing. Nor is it a good idea to argue over nonessential issues. Nevertheless, guarding the truth from error is a good fight worthy of our attention.

CHAPTER 8 STUDY QUESTIONS

1. **The Bible has been wrongly used to promote racism. What are some other examples of a good thing being wrongly used?**

There are many examples of good things being used for bad. An atomic bomb uses the energy from nuclear reactions to create massive destruction. Although the outcome is horrific, nobody would claim that all atoms are inherently bad because they can be misused for war. Wine is a good gift from God to gladden the heart (Psalm 104:15). However, this good gift can be wrongly used when excess leads to drunkenness, alcoholism, or driving under the influence. Misusing something does not make it inherently bad.

2. **Why is it so important to recognize the difference between description and prescription when reading the Bible?**

If these distinctions are overlooked, then you will likely end up with some awfully strange readings of the Bible. For instance, if you read the account of Noah and the flood as prescriptive, then you might go out and build a boat. In actuality, this narrative is describing how God worked to preserve Noah and his family through the flood. Similarly, to read Jesus' prescription for you to love your neighbor as descriptive will lead you to dismiss these words in your own life.

3. **Since Solomon enslaved certain people—and it's in the Bible!—does this mean that it is all right for other people to do it?**

No. Just because something is mentioned in the Bible does not mean that it is automatically permissible. The Bible also mentions instances of lying, murder, and incest. Claiming that because something is in the Bible it is therefore all right for people to do it is an extremely immature reading of Scripture.

4. **Scripture makes it clear that God's love is radically open to all people (Isaiah 56:1–8; Mark 16:15; Galatians 3:28). How are these verses even more powerful when placed in their historical context?**

These verses are powerful today. However, we live in a culture where racism and bigotry are viewed as negatives. In the ancient world, racial inequality was the standard expectation among many people. Situating these verses in their historical context makes them even more radical; when the rest of the world was advocating racism, the Bible was advocating God's love for all people.

5. **Why are religion and ethnicity often grouped together in Scripture?**

The notion of separating religion and ethnicity is a modern idea. Individual autonomy and the freedom to choose a religion separate from your nationality is a fairly recent invention. In the ancient world, it was assumed that the people of a nation worshiped the gods of that nation.

6. **What are some essential ways that God has relied on women in the Bible?**

Women are not secondary characters in Scripture. They have a leading role in many of God's fundamental promises and activities. These promises include the *Protoevangelium* and the promise that a woman would give birth to Jesus. The most climactic moment of the entire Bible, the resurrection of Jesus Christ, has women as the first eyewitnesses.

7. Does a difference in responsibilities automatically mean a difference in value?

Not at all! Just because God has ascribed different responsibilities to men and women, this does not mean that God values them differently. Both women and men have equal worth and value before God. In the same way, the persons of the Trinity—Father, Son, and Holy Spirit—are equally divine yet have different responsibilities and even demonstrate submission.

CHAPTER 9 STUDY QUESTIONS

1. **What do you think is the most outlandish claim in all of Scripture?**

There are many outlandish claims in the Bible. Perhaps the most central are the incarnation of Jesus Christ and His resurrection after being in the tomb for three days. However, beyond these there are many more: creation in six days, the Nile flowing with blood, Jonah living inside a fish, and Jesus healing many broken bodies. It is important to note that simply because a claim is outlandish or extraordinary does not mean it is automatically false or fabricated.

2. **How is it harder to disbelieve the miracles of Jesus than it is to believe them?**

Disbelieving the miracles of Jesus means disproving all the evidence supporting these occurrences. Not only is there evidence in the Bible supporting the miracles of Jesus, but there is also external evidence from nonbiblical historians testifying to His reputation for performing miracles. Furthermore, one has to explain away the fact that Jesus created such a stir with His public ministry (miracles included) that the religious leaders were motivated to kill Him. Disbelieving the miracles of Jesus requires one to deconstruct the supporting evidence and create a plausible explanation for how Jesus was able to hoodwink so many people.

3. **Why do people often want to make salvation more complicated than it is?**

Experience tells us that the more complicated something is, the more valuable it must be. Cars, computers, and cancer treatment are both complicated and valuable. We often import this sort of thinking into Scripture and attempt to overcomplicate salvation.

If God's plan of salvation is profoundly complex, then it must be valuable. This is not at all how the Bible depicts God's plan of salvation: we are saved by grace alone through faith alone in Christ Jesus.

4. If salvation in the Old Testament was not based on sacrifices, then why would God command them?

Salvation has never been based on the blood of goats or bulls. God's plan of salvation has always depended on the once-and-for-all sacrifice of Jesus (Hebrews 10:1–18). God commanded sacrifices in the Old Testament in order to give His people an outward sign of His mercy. God used the blood of the lamb at Passover to demonstrate His love and deliver His grace.

5. "All religions are essentially about being a good person." How does this statement misrepresent the message of Scripture?

The Bible is not about being a good person. It is about the goodness of God coming into this world in the person of Jesus Christ. Describing the Bible as a handbook on morality is a misunderstanding of God's Word. If Scripture has anything to do with being a good person, then it is about how God has come into your life in the person of Jesus Christ and made you a good person. This is hardly what people mean when they say that all religions are about being a good person.

6. If the Bible is about the life, death, and resurrection of Jesus, then does that mean it does not offer any guidance at all?

The Bible certainly offers guidance for living according to God's will. Many books in the Bible (e.g., Proverbs and Ecclesiastes) offer guidance for life. Furthermore, many of the epistles in the

New Testament offer guidance for how to live out your new life in Christ within the Church. Nevertheless, the Bible is not primarily a handbook on how to live. It is far more than a guide to living the good life. It is first and foremost God's proclamation of the good news of Jesus Christ.

7. **Why is it so outrageous by modern standards to claim that the Bible is right and every other holy book is wrong?**

Relativism claims that all truth is relative to the individual; what is true for me is not true for you. Many people have ironically accepted relativism as universally true. Claiming that one holy book is absolutely right and all others are to some degree wrong flies in the face of relativism. However, God's Word gives no indication that it should be accepted as one of many holy books. God makes it clear that His Word is true, authoritative, and life-giving.

SUGGESTED READING LIST

Metzger, Bruce Manning. *The New Testament: Its Background, Growth, and Content*. Nashville, TN: Abingdon Press, 1978.

This book is written by one of the greatest modern biblical scholars. It provides a historical and cultural context for understanding the New Testament. This is a challenging read aimed at a scholarly audience.

Eschelbach, Michael. *The Big Book of New Testament Questions and Answers*. St. Louis, MO: Concordia Publishing House, 2015.

This book helps readers understand the New Testament in greater detail. Many common questions about the Bible are discussed in this book. It is helpful to use this book alongside your daily Bible readings.

Burgland, Lane A. *Reading the Bible with Understanding*. St. Louis, MO: Concordia Publishing House, 1998.

This book provides a broad overview of biblical hermeneutics. Topics such as literary genre, linguistics, and interpretation of the Bible are explored in an accessible way. It's a valuable book for learning basic hermeneutics.

Walton, John H. *Ancient Israelite Literature in Its Cultural Context: A Survey of Parallels Between Biblical and Ancient Near Eastern Texts*. Grand Rapids, MI: Zondervan, 1994.

Drawing on modern archaeological findings, this book provides an introduction to literature and culture in the ancient Near East. This book gives readers a better understanding of how the Old Testament is unique when compared to other texts from the same time and place.

Strobel, Lee. *The Case for the Real Jesus: A Journalist Investigates Current Attacks on the Identity of Christ*. Grand Rapids, MI: Zondervan, 2007.

This book defends the historical reliability of the New Testament. It is an apologetic against the many claims that the history in the Bible does not accurately depict the real Jesus.

WHY SHOULD I TRUST THE BIBLE?

Lessing, R. Reed, and Andrew E. Steinmann. *Prepare the Way of the Lord: An Introduction to the Old Testament.* St. Louis, MO: Concordia Publishing House, 2014.

This book helps readers understand the Old Testament in greater detail. It provides a scholarly examination of the major themes in the Old Testament and is helpful for understanding the overall cohesion of the Bible.

Maier, Paul L. *In the Fullness of Time: A Historian Looks at Christmas, Easter, and the Early Church.* Grand Rapids, MI: Kregel Publications, 1997.

Written by one of the foremost scholars of ancient history, this book provides a historical context for the life of Jesus and the Early Church. This book provides a rich understanding of culture within the Greco-Roman world.

GLOSSARY

antilegomena. Biblical texts that some disagreed about in regards to their canonical status. There were some church leaders or congregations that did not consider these texts a part of the biblical canon because there were questions about author, content, or usage among congregations. Some examples of these books are the Epistle of James, Jude, and 2 Peter.

autograph. The original biblical text written by a divinely inspired author. The autographs were copied and reproduced in order to share the writings with many people.

canonization. The process of determining which books should be included in the Bible. Although this process was performed by the Early Church, it was done under the influence of the Holy Spirit. The Holy Spirit inspired the biblical authors before they wrote, while they were writing, and after they had written, ensuring that the right texts were included in the biblical canon.

dynamic equivalence. This Bible translation methodology aims at translating the intended message of the Bible from one language and culture to another. According to this methodology, translators aim to preserve the *thought* of the text in the translation. This means that wording may be slightly changed in order to capture the meaning of the original text.

evangelion. A Greek word that means "good news." This is translated into the English word *Gospel.*

formal correspondence. This methodology attempts to create a correspondence between the words in the source language and the target language.

functional equivalence. This methodology attempts to make the translation function in the target language as the original did in the source language.

general revelation. Knowledge of God that comes through nature, philosophy, or human reasoning. General revelation is silent when it comes to revealing God's plan of salvation.

heretical. Texts that were unanimously agreed upon as not fit to be included in the biblical canon because they were incorrect, inaccurate, or part of an entirely separate religious community. Some examples of these texts include the Gospel of Peter, the Gospel of Thomas, and the Acts of Andrew.

hermeneutics. A theory and methodology committed to properly interpreting Scripture. The goal of hermeneutics is to answer the question, "What does this mean?"

historical-critical method. This method of interpretation assumes that the Bible is a purely human text and the aim of interpretation should be to understand the historical factors that gave rise to the writing. This treats the Bible like any other work of literature.

historical-grammatical method. This method of interpretation strives to accurately understand the author's original meaning for the text. According to this method, the goal of biblical interpretation is to draw on reputable scholarship—history, archaeology, and ancient languages—in order to determine the meaning of the text as the original author and audience would have intended.

homologoumena. Texts that were unanimously included in the biblical canon. There were no disputes or disagreements as to whether these texts deserved to be in the Bible based on author, content, and widespread usage among congregations. Some examples of these books include the four Gospels, the Acts of the Apostles, and the Epistles of Paul.

lectio brevior. Latin for "shorter reading." This principle of textual criticism asserts that the shorter reading is most likely the closest to the original text.

lectio difficilior potior. Latin for "the more difficult reading is stronger." This principle of textual criticism asserts that the more difficult reading is most likely closest to the original text.

manuscript witnesses. The copies produced from the original autograph. There is only one autograph for each book of the Bible; however, there are many different manuscript witnesses.

paraphrasing. Attempting to make the Bible as readable and understandable as possible. This is also known as an idiomatic translation. In order to accomplish this, large departures from the original text are made for the sake of readability.

Protoevangelium. A foundational promise of God made in Genesis 3:15. This promise of God was made to Adam and Eve and pointed to the coming of Jesus Christ. This was the first mention of the Gospel made in Scripture.

pseudepigraphic. A text falsely attributed to an author.

relativism. This branch of philosophy claims that true and untrue, right and wrong, fact and fiction are strictly confined to the context that gives rise to them. What is true for one person is not true for another.

special revelation. God's direct revelation spoken to His creation. This includes the words of Jesus, the revelation of God spoken through prophets, and Scripture.

synoptic. The word means "similar" or "same view." The Synoptic Gospels—Matthew, Mark, and Luke—view the life and ministry of Jesus in the same way. This is compared to the Gospel of John, which has a different aim, placing a higher emphasis on the eternal truths of Jesus rather than linear history.

textual variants. When two manuscript witnesses do not agree with each other in some way. These discrepancies can be a missing word, change in spelling, or altered sentence order.